225

PRONUNCIATION EXERCISES

in

ENGLISH

(Revised Edition)

**Including Drills for the Correction
of Faulty Accent and Intonation**

By
M. ELIZABETH CLAREY
and
ROBERT J. DIXSON

A REGENTS PUBLICATION

Published by
Regents Publishing Company, Inc.
2 Park Avenue.
New York, N.Y. 10016

Library of Congress Catalog Card Number: 50-26005

Printed in the United States of America

TABLE OF CONTENTS

(Consonants)

Page

TABLE OF CONTENTS—*Continued*

(Vowels and Diphthongs)

PREFACE

THE TEACHING OF PRONUNCIATION*

The teaching of English pronunciation is both a simple and a complicated procedure. It is simple in that such teaching involves merely the drilling of students on the various sounds of English. Any conscientious teacher, who herself has good pronunciation, can do this. She offers herself as a model of good pronunciation, correcting as best she can any errors which the students make.

The teacher should keep in mind at all times, of course, that ear training is extremely important in the teaching of any foreign language. Drill on proper articulation of sounds is necessary, but ear training is even more fundamental. A student must first hear a sound clearly before he can reproduce it. Concepts of quality, pitch, and volume originate in the hearing area of the brain. The tonal image is heard mentally before it is actually produced by the voice. If this image is not exact, the production of the sound will not be accurate. Consequently, all pronunciation drills should be continued over as long a period of time as possible. The teacher should never jump from one exercise to another but should continue working on each individual sound until the sound is heard clearly by the students and the proper ear and hearing habits have been established.

On the other hand, although the teaching of pronunciation through mere imitation is an easy method to follow, such teaching can be, at the same time, a much more specialized task. If a teacher is to do more than simply guide her students through the various sounds, she should first understand some of the basic principles of English speech production. She should also be able to make use of these principles in her teaching. In this case, the effectiveness of her teaching does not depend so much upon the teaching methods or techniques which she employs but rather upon her knowledge and understanding of the general subject matter.

In this introduction on *Pronunciation*, we should like to discuss briefly some of the aspects of English speech which relate particularly to the correction of foreign accent.

---

* The material which follows is derived almost entirely from Chapter VII, The Teaching of Pronunciation, of *Practical Guide to the Teaching of English as a Foreign Language*, by Robert J. Dixson.

Phonetics—The International Phonetic Alphabet.

Phonetics has been defined as the study of speech sounds and the art of pronunciation. Any teacher who attempts to teach pronunciation, automatically makes some use of phonetics. The teacher's knowledge of theoretical phonetics may be very limited but, in correcting the accent of her foreign students, she unconsciously makes use of whatever she knows. She guides her students toward correct pronunciation through frequent drill. She makes careful distinction between one sound and another. All of this is phonetics. A distinction should be made here, of course, between *phonetics* and *phonetic symbols.* These terms are not identical although many people tend to use them indiscriminately. While phonetics is concerned with the study of speech sounds and proper pronunciation, phonetic symbols remain simply one of the tools which the phoneticist uses in analyzing language. It is quite possible to teach pronunciation without making use of phonetic symbols. It is also possible to make extensive use of such symbols without succeeding in teaching pronunciation.

The most common set of phonetic symbols now in use are those which make up the alphabet of the International Phonetic Association. Most teachers of English as a foreign language are already familiar with this International Phonetic Alphabet (IPA). Phonetic symbols of this alphabet now appear, in greater or lesser degree, in most modern textbooks. The language teacher's problem, generally, is to determine the extent to which she should make use of these IPA symbols in her own teaching.

Some teachers make extensive use of phonetic symbols and find them very useful in their teaching. In some cases, the extent to which such symbols are used depends upon the particular class situation. In a well organized school system where students begin to study English in the lower grades and continue the study of English for several years, there is both time and opportunity to make phonetics an integral part of the program. In shorter, more intensive courses there is often little space left for phonetic transcriptions of any kind. Many teachers, moreover, are not sufficiently trained to use the IPA system efficiently. Students in some circumstances react unfavorably to learning phonetic symbols of any kind.

The theory underlying the use of phonetic symbols is, of course, simple and logical. The International Phonetic Alphabet provides a single symbol for each sound in the language. In English, for example, where the pronunciation of a word so often fails to accord with the spelling, we thus have a method of making the pronunciation clear. Particularly in cases where a student cannot pronounce a word or is confused by the obscuring of certain syllables, it is helpful to be able to transcribe the word into phonetic script. Also, in teaching certain of the vowel sounds—particularly those which are peculiar to English—it is useful to have at hand a symbol to represent these sounds. By means of phonetic symbols one can also indicate the voicing or unvoicing of terminal consonants, the existence of strong and weak forms, etc. These are all definite advantages.

Yet, despite these advantages, as one goes down through the ranks of practicing teachers, one finds considerable disenchantment with the entire phonetic system of transcription, now in use. Many teachers have conscientiously tried to use the IPA system in their work, only to find that the results did not justify the time spent, first, in teaching the various symbols themselves and, second, in adapting these symbols to the many subtleties of everyday English speech. Moreover, attempts to simplify the IPA system have not been particularly successful. One group of authorities have sponsored one set of changes, another group have recommended something quite different. While the general tendency toward simplification is to be commended, such unrelated changes only add to the confusion already felt by many teachers regarding the use of phonetic symbols in general.

Finally, the phonetic symbols in current school use, *without special qualifying markings*, fail to indicate in any way important differences between the production of many English sounds and the production of the corresponding sounds in other languages. English *t*, for example, is not pronounced like Spanish *t*. English *p* is not pronounced like Spanish *p*. The sounds *t, d, p, b, k, g* are all aspirated in English and produced with a slightly different tongue position from that used in Spanish. English *l* and English *r* have little similarity to Spanish *l* and Spanish *r*. Yet the current phonetic symbols for *t, d, p, b, k, g, r, l* indicate no differences between the two corresponding sets of sounds. Consequently, the English-speaking person will give to these symbols his own English pronunciation; the Spanish-speaking person will give them a Spanish pronunciation—and each one will assume that he is pronouncing the sounds correctly in the foreign language.

Classification of Speech Sounds

There are twenty six letters in the English alphabet but upwards of

9

some fifty different and distinct sounds. It is not our purpose or province here to describe all of these sounds or even to attempt to classify each of them. What follows below is merely a very general outline of the most important classes of English sounds. Some of the terms defined here appear frequently in later discussions. Therefore, we will describe such terms briefly at this point in order that the reader may understand more easily the material which follows. Any teacher who is interested in learning more about this general subject matter is referred to the various standard textbooks dealing with English speech.

The sounds of any language are generally divided into two main groups—vowels and consonants. All vowels are produced with voice, that is, with vibration of the vocal cords. They differ from consonants in that the outward flow of sound is largely unrestricted. In consonants, this flow is interrupted or diverted by one of the articulators—teeth, tongue, lips, soft palate.

There are anywhere from eleven to sixteen vowels in English, depending upon their classification. That is, the number depends not upon their possible production within the speech apparatus but upon their classification by different phoneticians. Some writers on phonetics recognize three vowels in the *a* group and four in the mid-vowel group. More recent writers tend toward some simplification of these and other groups. Phoneticians further classify vowels as *front, middle,* and *back* vowels, depending upon the position of the tongue in the mouth during production. Thus, [i], [ɪ], and [e] are front vowels, the tongue being in high front position when they are produced; [u], [ʊ], and [o] are back vowels; [ə] and [ɝ] are middle vowels.

Consonants are classified according to the manner of articulation as follows: (1) Stops or plosives. In the production of these sounds, the breath is checked in its outward movement, then suddenly released with a slight explosion. In this group fall the sounds *p, b, t, d, k, g.* (2) Continuants. A continuant is a sound which may be "continued" or prolonged as long as the speaker has breath to sustain it. Continuants are further divided into nasals [m, n, and ŋ]. laterals [l], and fricatives [f, v, h, w, θ, ð, s, z, ʃ, ʒ].

A further classification of consonants concerns their production with voice or with voiceless breath. This is an important classification for our purposes since the voicing or unvoicing of consonants, under certain specified conditions, is important in foreign accent correction. *Voiced consonants* are produced with vibration of the vocal chords. In this group we have *b, d, g, l, ð, v, z, ʒ*. *Unvoiced consonants* are produced with breath alone. These include *p, t, k, θ, ʃ, s, ʃ*.

It should be further observed that most voiced and unvoiced consonants fall into pairs, one consonant of the pair being voiced and the other unvoiced. Thus *b* is voiced; *p* is unvoiced—although both sounds are otherwise produced alike. Such pairs may be grouped as follows:

Voiced	b	d	g	v	z	ð	ʒ
Unvoiced	p	t	k	f	s	θ	ʃ

Stress and Rhythm—Strong and Weak Forms

Stress is the emphasis given to a particular syllable within a word or to a particular word within a group of words. In individual words, stress is generally referred to as *accent*.

In English, as is generally known, words are very strongly accented. The accented syllable receives greater force than in most languages. The unaccented syllables, in turn, receive correspondingly less force. This tendency in English results in various phonetic changes. In emphasizing the accented syllable so strongly, we automatically sacrifice the vowel values in the remaining unstressed syllables. *It may be stated as a principle in English that all vowels, when occurring in unstressed syllables, are reduced from their normal values to the level of the neutral vowel* [ə]. For example, in the words attempt [ətɛ́mpt], contain [kəntén], we can see clearly how this principle operates. The vowel of the unaccented syllable in each case is reduced from its normal value to the neutral [ə]. The only vowels which seem to resist this leveling tendency on occasion are the high front vowel [i] and the low back vowel [u]. Both these vowels are also reduced in unstressed syllables, but [i] is sometimes weakened only to [ɪ], as in *become* [bɪkə́m]; [u] is weakened to [ʊ], as in *July* [dʒʊláɪ].

This important principle of English speech is often difficult for the foreign student to understand. In his native language, the student is often taught to respect the quality of all vowels. So, in speaking English, he naturally assumes that if he pronounces each syllable clearly and exactly he will be better understood. Actually, the reverse is true. Words in English are distinguishable by rhythm as well as by sound. Consequently the student will be much better understood if he stresses the accented syllable strongly and totally obscures all remaining vowels.

11

Although consonants do not have strong and weak forms, they also undergo changes in value, just as vowels do. They are subject to the influence of stress. They are also influenced particularly by neighboring sounds, undergoing a process known as *assimilation*. Thus one sound may be altered by the sound which follows it (progressive assimilation). Another sound may be altered by the sound which precedes it (regressive assimilation). In the word *looked,* for example, the final voiced *d* follows a breathed *k*. After pronouncing *k*, it is so much easier for us to leave the vocal cords in relaxed position rather than to draw them together sharply for the normal voicing of the *d* that we end up by unvoicing the *d*. The word, though still retaining its old spelling, is thus pronounced [lʊkt].

Actually, assimilation is a very common process, occurring in all languages. It results from a simple *law of economy,* whereby the organs of speech, instead of taking a new position for each sound, tend to draw sounds together with the purpose of saving time and energy. Assimilation becomes important in teaching English to foreign students only when the teacher fails to understand its operation and importance. Many teachers tend to follow the spelling of words and to teach overly-precise forms rather than accepted assimilations. Thus some teachers will teach *picture* as [píktyʊr] rather than [píktʃɚ]. By analogy they then teach *nature* as [nétyur] instead of [nétʃɚ], *literature* as [lítɚətyʊr] instead of [lítɚətʃɚ]. They teach *educate* as [ɛ́dyʊket] rather than [ɛ́dʒəket]. These same teachers are likely to claim that *did you,* pronounced [dídʒʊ], or *don't you,* pronounced [dóntʃʊ] are vulgarisms to be avoided in careful speech. Yet these forms occur in their own speech and in the speech of everyone who speaks everyday, normal English. Students, therefore, should be acquainted with these and comparable assimilations. Even if they can't use them in their own speech, they should at least be able to recognize and understand them in the speech of others.

We read above that all words of more than one syllable are strongly accented in English. That is, one syllable receives considerable stress while the remaining syllables are weakened accordingly. *This same principle of accent holds true in phrases as well as in individual words.* In all phrases, in English, one word or syllable is strongly accented. The remaining words or syllables receive correspondingly less stress. The vowels in all unstressed syllables are reduced from their original values to the neutral vowel [ə]. One syllable words such as articles, conjunctions, and pronouns are reduced to their corresponding *weak forms.* The article *an* [æn], for example, is weakened to [ən]. The conjunction *and* [ænd] becomes [ənd], *can* [kæn] becomes [kən] or even [kn]—etc.

It is easy for students (and teachers) to understand the accenting of individual words—but rarely do they understand the comparable accenting of phrases or thought groups. Yet when we speak, we always speak in phrases, not words. It is quite natural that we should accent the main or content words in a sentence and subordinate the less important elements.

It so happens that almost any phrase in English can be compared in its accent to some individual word. Thus, the phrase *in the morning* [ɪnðəmórnɪŋ] is accented exactly as the word *economic* [ɪkənámɪk]. The phrase *he's leaving* [hizlívɪŋ] carries the same accent as the word *appearing* [əpírɪŋ]. *"I'll be there"* [ɑɪlbɪðέr] compares exactly in accent to *disappear* [dɪsəpír]. *"He's been working"* [hizbɪnwə́kɪŋ] is accented in the same way as the word *introduction* [ɪntrədə́kʃən]. A long list of such equally accented phrases and individual words can be drawn up by the teacher and used by the students for practice purposes.

Obviously, in special circumstances, one can alter the pattern of any phrase and emphasize a different word or syllable from the one normally stressed. If someone asks us, "Is the book *on* the table or *under* the table?" we might well reply "ON the table," stressing *on* rather than the first syllable of *table*, which is usually stressed. But this is a special situation which does not concern us here. *Remember this:* In normal, everyday, colloquial speech all phrases carry a definite accent. Moreover, this accent, which grows out of the grammar of the language, is recurrent and stable. Thus any two native speakers of English, under normal circumstances, will read the same phrase in exactly the same way. In brief, to the English ear, the accent of any phrase is as clear and recognizable as the accent of any individual word. Finally—*and this is a very important point*—if any phrase is accented incorrectly, the error is just as great and just as obvious as when a word is accented on the wrong syllable.

Many times a foreign student, trying to be precise, will say, for example, "I *am* busy," putting stress on *am* instead of on the first syllable of *busy*, where it normally goes. The resulting distortion is just as clear to the English ear (and just as confusing) as if the student, in pronouncing the word *Indiana* [ɪndiǽna] mistakenly shifted the accent to the second syllable and said instead InDIana [ɪndiǿnə].

What we are discussing here is really rhythm. The succession of properly accented phrases in a sentence establishes what is known as the rhythm of a language. Rhythm is a definite and tangible phase of language. Rhythm provides a kind of musical framework for language. More important still, it also helps to convey meaning. In many cases rhythm is as important in this respect as individual words or grammar.

The teacher may well ask how she should go about teaching stress and rhythm—if they have this importance. Clearly, she should not neglect more fundamental things to concentrate on stress and rhythm. Rhythm is a rather subtle matter. It is not easily grasped or appreciated by students, particularly on the elementary or lower intermediate levels. Yet there are a few obvious things which the teacher, if she is interested, can do. First, she can show the relation between the accenting of many common phrases and individual words—as explained above. In this connection she should be sure to emphasize the fact that we speak in phrases, not words, and that all phrases carry a definite accent, just as words do. The special exercises in this book on the proper stressing of phrases should prove helpful to the teacher in this respect. Secondly, the teacher can teach phrasing as part of the teaching of pronunciation. In reading practice sentences to the class, she can emphasize the stressing of accented syllables and the obscuring of vowels in all unaccented syllables. Students, in repeating such sentences after her, should follow the same rhythm patterns which she has emphasized. Again, the intonation exercises which appear in each lesson of this book should help to give the students the "feel" of most of the patterns into which English rhythm naturally falls. Thirdly, the teacher can make use of the device of rhyming—particularly in teaching contracted verb forms such as *I'm, you're, we're, I'll, she'll, we've, etc.* Students fail to contract many of these forms sufficiently. They pronounce them as though they were composed of two syllables rather than a single syllable. The teacher can counteract this tendency by showing that *I'll* rhymes with *pile. He's* rhymes with *sneeze. I'm* rhymes with *time. We've* rhymes with *leave*—and so on. Fourthly, the teacher can show students how English rhythm falls into certain definite patterns. These patterns grow out of the grammar of English, in accordance with the following general principles: *In speaking, we naturally stress so-called content words.* In most sentences, such words carry the burden of meaning. They include: *nouns, main verbs, descriptive adjectives, adverbs, demonstratives* (this, that, these, those), *interrogatives* (who, which, why, when, etc.)

In turn we subordinate all functional words, words which serve simply to define or show mood, direction, etc. The following are considered functional words in English and, accordingly, are normally unstressed:

definite and indefinite articles (a, an, the), *personal pronouns* (I, you, he, my, your, his, etc.), *auxiliary verbs* (am, are, is, will, have, may, can, etc.), *relative pronouns* (who, which, that, whom), *conjunctions* (and, but, although, if, etc.)

Intonation

Intonation is the term used to describe the pitch or melody pattern of any group of words. The group of words involved is sometimes known as the "intonation group." Pitch, in case the term is not familiar to the reader, is the position of a note on the musical scale. Pitch is determined by the frequency of vibration at which air waves strike the ear drum.

Very often, when there is an increase of stress on any one syllable, there is an accompanying rise in pitch on the same syllable. However, one should be careful to distinguish clearly between stress and pitch. Stress is associated with rhythm. Variations in stress give rise to rhythm in language. Stress patterns and the resultant rhythm, as we have seen, grow out of the grammar of a language. Thus rhythm is stable and fairly predictable.

Changes in pitch, on the other hand, result in varying intonation patterns. Pitch is often a personal or individual matter—especially on advanced levels. Pitch and the resultant intonation thus show a great variation in form. In addition, they frequently carry various emotional overtones.

The following two principles govern all basic intonation patterns in English. Actually, these two principles are really all any foreign student needs to know about intonation and all he needs to be taught:

1. The first principle requires that all completed statements, including commands, end with a downward glide of the voice on the last accented syllable. This type of intonation is known as Rising-Falling intonation. It is used for all statements and commands. The fall of the voice at the end of a sentence indicates to the listener that the speaker has terminated and no answer or further comment is necessarily expected.

2. The second principle is that all statements indicating incompleteness, doubt, or hesitation end with an upward glide of the voice on the last accented syllable. In this category are included all questions which may be answered *yes* or *no*. This type of intonation is known as Rising intonation. Questions beginning with interrogative words such as *When,*

15

Where, *Why*, since these words in themselves indicate that the statement is a question, generally follow the first principle.

In this book, the following system of intonation is used: There are three tones involved—normal, high, and low. A line drawn directly at the base of a word shows that the word is pronounced with a normal tone; a line just above the word indicates a high tone; a line well below the level of a word indicates a low tone.

a) The following are examples of type one intonation—that is, Rising-Falling intonation. Note that the high note generally coincides with the last stressed syllable of the sentence.

The boy is lazy.

What time will you call me?

Note that in some of the sentences where Rising-Falling intonation occurs the last sentence stress may fall on a word of only one syllable. In such cases there is no room for the low note to follow. An inflection of the voice then occurs, indicated by a curved line.

She didn't say a word.

Come back soon.

b) The following is an example of type two intonation—namely, Rising intonation.

Will you return later?

Does he plan to take it with him?

Aspiration

Aspiration is the term given to the slight puff of air, like an [h], which follows the production of [p], [t], and [k] in English. This aspiration is strongest when [p], [t], and [k] are in initial position and followed by a vowel, as in the word *pen* [pɛn]. It is next strongest when the sounds are in final position after a consonant as in *sent* [sɛnt]. It is weakest when the sounds occur in medial position; here the puff of air is so slight as to be hardly perceptible—as in *happy* [hæpɪ].

16

This aspiration is not a fundamental part of these sounds—which are all voiceless plosives. As may be seen from what has just been said, the aspiration varies in intensity with the position of the sound. When [p], [t], or [k] are followed by a consonant in the same breath group, the puff does not occur at all—Example: *pride* [praɪd]. Yet the aspiration remains a very important characteristic of each of these sounds, especially if the sound is in initial position. For one thing, the aspiration serves to distinguish the sounds from their voiced cognates [b], [d], and [g]. The sound [p], for example, is more than merely the unvoiced counterpart (cognate) of [b]. It is unvoiced [b], with a distinctive aspiration added —and this aspiration is clearly noticeable to the English ear and helps substantially in identifying the sound.

The same aspiration of these sounds does not occur in German, in the Slavic languages, or in any of the Romance languages. Consequently most foreign students studying English pay little attention to it. Generally the student does not hear the aspiration clearly. Even in cases where he may hear it, he is unable to reproduce it. Yet no error is more noticeable in the speech of foreign students. It is an error which clings to the speech of even the most advanced students.

To the person not trained in speech, the difference between an aspirated [t] and an unaspirated [t] may not seem a very significant one. Yet the failure to aspirate comes through very clearly in English speech, causing a heavy, blunt effect which is definitely non-English. Compare the pronounciation of *ten* (the numeral) in English and *ten* (the imperative form of *tener*) in Spanish. There sometimes results a definite confusion of words if the necessary aspiration is lacking. In rapid speech, unaspirated [p] sounds like voiced [b]; unaspirated [t] sounds like [d]; unaspirated [k] like [g]. The foreign student says *ten* without aspirating the [t], and the native listener thinks he is saying *den*. The foreign student says *pie* and it sounds to his native listener like *by*.

This error, in general, is fairly easy to correct once the teacher understands the principle involved and the facts are made clear to the students. The teacher should first show the students how strong is the aspiration of [p], [t], and [k] in her own speech. She should pass among the students repeating such words as *pen, ten, come.* She can exaggerate slightly the aspiration on [p], [t], and [k]—though this is not really neccesary since the aspiration on these sounds, even in normal speech, is considerable. She can let students feel with the backs of their hands the strong

17

puff of air which is emitted from her mouth each time she pronounces [p], [t], and [k]. Students are generally amazed at the really strong aspiration given to these sounds. Or the teacher can hold a small piece of paper lightly in front of her mouth as she speaks. The paper will flutter each time she says [p], [t], or [k]. A match flame, held before the mouth, shows the same effect.

After this, it is just a matter of practice on the students' part to learn this important principle of aspiration. Students should repeat aloud simple words beginning with [p]—*pen, pay, pour, put, pear*. Later they should practice with simple words beginning with [t] and [k]. At first, students can hold pieces of paper before their mouths to show the amount of aspiration taking place. However, this soon becomes unnecessary because the sharp difference between the aspirated and unaspirated forms of these sounds is presently clear to all. From this point on, it is just a matter of correction each time a student fails to aspirate [p], [t], or [k] sufficiently.

Voicing and Unvoicing of Final Consonants

Another serious error of the foreign student learning English is his failure, in required circumstances, to voice final consonants. We have already learned the difference between voiced and unvoiced consonants. (See page 11) The particular voiced consonants which concern us here are [b, d, g, v, z, ð, ʒ]. Their unvoiced counterparts are [p, t, k, f, s, θ, ʃ].

Sometimes in rapid speech it is difficult to tell whether a consonant is voiced or unvoiced. This simple test may be used. Stop the ears while sounding alternately any such pairs as *fife* and *five*, prolonging the final sounds of *f* and *v*. In holding the sound *f* by itself, one will hear only a fricative rustling of the breath as it passes the teeth and lips. In sounding *v*, this same friction is heard with the addition of voice, the vibration of the vocal cords.

In English, all voiced consonants, occurring at the end of a word are generally held and voiced. In German, the Slavic and Romance languages the opposite situation prevails. All voiced consonants, when occurring in terminal position, are automatically unvoiced. For example, in Russian the name *Chekhov*, although terminating in *v*, a voiced consonant, is pronounced [tʃɛ́kɔf]. In accordance with the rules of Russian, the final *v* is automatically unvoiced and changed into its unvoiced counterpart *f*. In English this same word would normally be pronounced [tʃɛ́kɔv]. The

18

final *v* would be held and voiced. Compare English pronunciation of *love* [ləv], *move* [muv], *of* [əv].

The foreign student, in bringing to English the habits of speech acquired in his own native language, naturally tends to unvoice all final voiced consonants. The effect in English, however, is unfortunate. The student, instead of saying *his* [hɪz] says [hɪs]. Instead of saying *have* [hæv], he says [hæf]. For *bag* [bæg], he says [bæk]—and so on. The list of such possible distortions, where the foreign student turns final *d* into *t*, final *g* into *k*, final *v* into *f* and so forth, is almost endless. In some cases, actual confusion of words results. If a student, in pronouncing *bad*, unvoices the final *d* and changes it to *t*, he comes out with *bat*. In such a case, he has changed not only the form of the word but also its meaning. There are many pairs of English words distinguishable only by the voicing or unvoicing of the final consonant. Consider—to name just a few: *bed, bet; need, neat; feed, feet; buzz, bus; grows, gross; rise, rice; raise, race; pays, pace; leave, leaf; bag, back.*

As may be readily seen, it is very important to hold and voice all such final voiced consonants in English. This voicing sometimes varies in intensity, but this fact need not concern the foreign student. The principles involved should first be explained to the student so that he understands what he is doing. Then he should be drilled carefully on matching pairs of words such as those which appear above. He should also be given practice with phrases and short sentences containing final voiced consonants. It is sometimes helpful if it is explained to the student that all vowels preceding final voiced consonants are somewhat lengthened in duration. That is, all vowels are held slightly longer before final voiced consonants than before final unvoiced consonants. The [æ] in *bad*, for example, is of longer duration than the [æ] in *bat*. The [ɛ] in *bed* is held longer than the [ɛ] of *bet*—etc.

INTERNATIONAL PHONETIC ALPHABET
CONSONANTS

[p] — pie, hope, happy

[b] — bell, bite, globe

[f] — fine, office

[v] — vest, of, have

[k] — keep, can, book

[g] — go, get, egg

[l] — let, little, lay

[m] — man, must, dime

[n] — no, down, ton

[ŋ] — sing, ringing

[w] — water, we, one

[θ] — thin, three, path

[ð] — they, then, other

[s] — see, sat, city

[z] — zoo, does, is

[ʃ] — shoe, ship, action

[ʒ] — usual, garage

[tʃ] — change, watch

[dʒ] — June, edge

[r] — red, rich, write

[y] — you, yes, million

[h] — he, hat, who

[t] — ten, to, meet

[d] — do, did, sudden

VOWELS AND DIPHTHONGS

[ɪ] — it, did, build

[i] — me, see, people

[ɛ] — end, let, any

[æ] — cat, bat, laugh

[ɑ] — army, father, hot

[ɔ] — all, caught, long

[ʊ] — book, full, took

[u] — too, move, fruit

[ə] — cup, soda, infant

[ɚ] — her, work, bird

[e] — say, they, mail

[o] — old, coal, sew

[ɑɪ] — dry, eye, buy

[ɔɪ] — toy, boy, soil

[ɑʊ] — cow, our, house

NOTE: In accordance with common practice and for reasons of simplification, these minor changes in symbols have been introduced. [ə] and [ɚ] are used in this book for both stressed and unstressed syllables. [y] is used instead of IPA [j]. [ɑ] is used instead of IPA [a].

CONSONANTS

p as in pie, happy, hope

I. Production:

Close your lips, then blow them open with a puff of air, but without voice.

pear	people	top
pick	September	hip
pet	apple	pep
palm	purple	nap
part	complete	cap
poor	apartment	soup

II. Comparison

Practice these contrasting sounds, which are sometimes confused. Repeat several times.

bear—pear	big—pig
rib—rip	bath—path
cab—cap	bay—pay
be—pea	bet—pet

III. Sentences

1. The paper was printed and published without profit.
2. We had to learn both the past and present tense of all verbs.
3. Paula carefully put the apples and peaches in the basket.
4. Our plan was opposed by almost everyone present.
5. Drops of water kept dripping from the roof.
6. The umpire, now in bad temper, argued loudly with the player.
7. Both the interest and the principal must be paid in September.
8. His only hope of escape lay through the opening in the fence.

IV. Phrasing and Intonation

a. *Phrases:* Blend together the words in each of these phrases to form a single unit—that is, pronounce each phrase as though it were a single word. Also stress the accented syllable rather strongly, obscuring the vowels in the remaining syllables accordingly.

a bád puppy	a prétty bird	to pláy ball
a bíg puppy	to be próud	my bést cap
múch better prose	to táke a nap	in the párk

b. *Sentences:* The teacher reads each of the following sentences in a normal manner, giving some slight emphasis to phrasing and intonation. Students repeat after teacher. Teacher repeats after students.

1. (Teacher) They played in the ⌐park⌐ all afternoon.
   (Students) They played in the park all afternoon.
   (Teacher) They played in the park all afternoon.

2. (Teacher) Why didn't you ⌐buy⌐ some apples?
   (Students) Why didn't you buy some apples?
   (Teacher) Why didn't you buy some apples?

3. (Teacher) Do you prefer ⌐pork or beef?
   (Students) Do you prefer pork or beef?
   (Teacher) Do you prefer pork or beef?

Teacher and students continue in exactly the same manner with these sentences: Teacher reads, students repeat, teacher repeats.

4. Paul practiced playing the piano all morning.

23

5. I prefer peaches but Peter likes plums.

6. I don't play bridge but I like to watch others play.

7. What department does Peter work in?

8. Peter now works in the printing department.

9. Where did you buy that pretty play suit?

10. I bought it in Pratt's Department Store.

V. Review Paragraph

The Reverend Peter Parry, pastor of the First Episcopal Church, 22 Peach Street, Peekskill, New York, was making a telephone call to a friend of his, the Reverend Paul Porter, pastor of an Episcopal church in Pittsburgh, Pennsylvania.

"Is this a person to person call?" the operator asked Reverend Parry.

"No," said Reverend Parry. "This is parson to parson."

b as in **bell, rubber, globe**

I. Production:

Close the lips firmly, then open them, producing a voiced sound. Be sure no puff of air comes out.

be	about	job
big	rabbit	rib
bet	subscription	cab
bat	subtract	rob
barn	subject	robe
boot	able	rub

II. Comparison

rib—rip	by—pie
cab—cap	bill—pill
bark—park	bath—path
back—pack	ball—Paul

III. Sentences

1. The brass band played so loudly, we could barely hear each other.
2. The boys assembled in groups about a block apart.
3. The cab stopped at the curb and the cab driver jumped out.
4. It was too big a job for Benny to do.
5. The waitress brought us bread but no butter.
6. It was by far the best ball game of the season.
7. The boys hid behind the back fence.
8. The rabbit ran into a hole behind the barn.

IV. Phrasing and Intonation

a. *Phrases*: Blend together the words in each of these phrases to form a single unit—that is, pronounce each phrase as though it were a single word. Also stress the accented syllable rather strongly, obscuring the vowels in the remaining syllables acccordingly.

to búy a pencil	a bríght pin	pápa paid for it
to báke a pie	a páper bag	a bróken plate
to bé with the boys	a bíg bill	to pláy bridge

b. *Sentences*: The teacher reads each of the following sentences in a normal manner, giving some slight emphasis to phrasing and intonation. Students repeat after teacher. Teacher repeats after students.

1. (Teacher) Barbara was a very pretty bride.

   (Students) Barbara was a very pretty bride.

   (Teacher) Barbara was a very pretty bride.

2. (Teacher) What subject were they talking about?

   (Students) What subject were they talking about?

   (Teacher) What subject were they talking about?

3. (Teacher) Were you able to reach Mr. Brown?

   (Students) Were you able to reach Mr. Brown?

   (Teacher) Were you able to reach Mr. Brown?

Teacher and students continue in exactly the same manner with these sentences: Teacher reads, students repeat, teacher repeats.

4. Where did you buy those rubber boots?

5. I bought them in Brown's Department Store.
6. When is the boy's next birthday?
7. He was born in the month of February.
8. Have all the big bills for this month been paid?
9. Ben has a good job at the bank.
10. At the banquet I sat between Betty and Bob.

V. Review Paragraph

Every day the boys burst out of the building like a ball of fire. A moment before, everything had been quiet and peaceful in the school-yard. Now small boys, large boys, thin boys, fat boys, all descend in a big mob, taking full advantage of the brief assembly period. Back and forth they run, elbowing each other, playing ball or tag, beating each other over the head, pushing, pulling. One wonders why there are not more broken bones. The noise is so great that one can barely think. Then, finally, the bell rings. Sadly, the boys go back, one by one, into the building and to their books. The assembly period is over. The school-yard again takes on its peaceful, suburban air, and all is right once more with the world.

| **m** | as in **my, summer, palm** |

I. Production:

Press the lips tightly together and hum with voice.

man	company	some
men	empty	home
make	summer	time
may	games	come
me	famous	arm
my	almost	from

II. Comparison

Practice these contrasting sounds, which are sometimes confused. Repeat several times.

make—bake	some—sun
my—by	warm—warn
meet—beat	dime—dine
mean—bean	them—then

III. Sentences

1. They may remain here until March.
2. Martin's work may mean a good promotion for him in time.
3. He comes from a family of moderate income.
4. The smell of smoke was so strong, that many people began to move toward the exits.
5. His fame was limited to a few minor headlines in the daily papers.
6. He lives in a one-room apartment in the middle of town.
7. They walked home arm in arm.
8. The warm summer sun made everyone very uncomfortable.

IV. Phrasing and Intonation

a. *Phrases:* Blend together the words in each of these phrases to form a single unit—that is, pronounce each phrase as though it were a single word. Also stress the accented syllable rather strongly, obscuring the vowels in the remaining syllables accordingly.

among the bóoks	álmost everyone	will cóme later
bóth of them	to máke money	feels múch better
I may be láte	from tíme to time	at the sáme time

b. *Sentences:* The teacher reads each of the following sentences in a normal manner, giving some slight emphasis to phrasing and intonation. Students repeat after teacher. Teacher repeats after students.

1. (Teacher)   Have you|met my mother and brother ?

    (Students)   Have you met my mother and brother ?

    (Teacher)   Have you met my mother and brother ?

2. (Teacher)   No, but I'm very|glad|to meet them.

    (Students)   No, but I'm very glad to meet them.

    (Teacher)   No, but I'm very glad to meet them.

3. (Teacher)   Why don't you come to our|home|for dinner ?

    (Students)   Why don't you come to our home for dinner ?

    (Teacher)   Why don't you come to our home for dinner ?

Teacher and students continue in exactly the same manner with these sentences: Teacher reads, students repeat, teacher repeats.

4. I'd like to come very much.

5. May I offer you some lemonade ?
6. What was the name of that author we were speaking about ?
7. Do you mean Somerset Maugham, by any chance ?
8. Must the children make so much noise ?
9. What country do Mr. and Mrs. Martinez come from ?
10. They are Mexicans but have lived for many years in Montana.

V. Review Paragraph

Mr. Morris Markey, a merchant of Manhattan, was teaching his young son, Max, the dry-goods business.

"Climb up that ladder," said Mr. Markey to Max.

Max climbed carefully to the top of the ladder.

"Now jump, Max, and Father will catch you," said Mr. Markey, arms outstretched, as he motioned to Max.

"But I'm afraid," Max said.

"Jump," said Mr. Markey more firmly, "and Father will catch you."

Max jumped. Mr. Markey stepped aside. Max struck the floor heavily.

"That is the first lesson in business, Max," said Mr. Markey. "Never trust anyone."

hw as in why, whisper, somewhere

I. Production:

Round your lips and blow out, making a voiceless sound.

which	whiskers	nowhere
where	whiskey	somewhere
why	whisper	anywhere
when	whip	somewhat
what	whether	meanwhile
white	whistle	everywhere

II. Comparison

Practice these contrasting sounds, which are sometimes confused. Repeat several times.

which—witch	where—hair
whether—weather	when—hen
what—watt	wheat—heat
where—wear	white—height

III. Sentences

1. The white snow fell softly to the ground.
2. Where and when did William get such an idea?
3. His well-cut white whiskers gave him a distinguished look.
4. Wherever he went and whatever he did, his reputation remained everywhere the same.
5. Meanwhile, the books which we had been waiting for were delivered somewhere else.
6. We whistled and whistled, but were not sure whether anyone heard us.
7. No one knew when or why he had left.
8. In the story of Moby Dick, Captain Ahab looks everywhere for the white whale.

IV. Phrasing and Intonation

a. *Phrases*: Blend together the words in each of these phrases to form a single unit—that is, pronounce each phrase as though it were a single word. Also stress the accented syllable rather strongly, obscuring the vowels in the remaining syllables accordingly.

whíte wine	sómewhat wet	whíte whiskers
whát to do	whích way is west ?	whén and where
why wáit for her?	whát's the matter?	why wórry about it?

b. *Sentences*: The teacher reads each of the following sentences in a normal manner, giving some slight emphasis to phrasing and intonation. Students repeat after teacher. Teacher repeats after students.

1. (Teacher)   Which do you prefer—white wine or red ?

   (Students) Which do you prefer—white wine or red ?

   (Teacher)   Which do you prefer—white wine or red ?

2. (Teacher)   Have you decided what to do ?

   (Students) Have you decided what to do ?

   (Teacher)   Have you decided what to do ?

3. (Teacher)   He painted all the woodwork white.

   (Students) He painted all the woodwork white.

   (Teacher)   He painted all the woodwork white.

Teacher and students continue in exactly the same manner with these sentences: Teacher reads, students repeat, teacher repeats.

4. I don't see our waiter anywhere.

5. What is the name of the man with the white whiskers ?
6. What were Mr. and Mrs. White doing meanwhile ?
7. Why didn't you call us when you felt ill ?
8. Which is the 75 watt bulb ?

V. Review Paragraph

The initial sound in such words as *where, which,* and *what* is produced with a slight puff of air—like an *h* sound. This *h* sound may be noticed if a piece of paper is held before the lips. Each time words like *where, which,* and *what* are spoken, the paper will move slightly. No such puff of air is noticed when corresponding words without the *h* sound are spoken—words such as *wear, witch,* and *watt.* We may say, therefore, that this slight puff of air helps to distinguish between *where* and *wear, which* and *witch, what* and *watt.*

On the other hand, it should be pointed out that the substitution of *w* for *wh* is not a serious error in English. Many Americans and many British people make no distinction at all between *which* and *witch, where* and *wear, whether* and *weather.* Also in rapid speech, the *h* sound tends to disappear even in the speech of those who normally introduce an *h* sound in these particular words. One may argue that some confusion may result if no difference is made, for example, between *whether* and *weather* or between *what* and *watt.* But one can generally tell from the context which word is meant. In fact, in English, there are literally hundreds of so-called homonyms—that is, sets of words which are spelled differently but pronounced alike. These include words such as *scene, seen; son, sun; one, won; night, knight.* Many of these homonyms are very common words; they are used frequently in English—yet little confusion results because, again, the context in which the words appear generally makes clear their meaning immediately.

W as in **water, one, quite**

I. Production:

Push the lips forward and blow out with a voiced sound.

west	weather	away
way	won	twenty
work	wise	awake
wide	water	forward
warm	went	backward
wind	word	between

II. Comparison

Practice these contrasting sounds, which are sometimes confused. Repeat several times.

west—vest	wait—rate
wine—vine	wise—rise
worse—verse	won—run
went—vent	wipe—ripe

III. Sentences

1. We decided to wait one week for Warren's answer.
2. A warm wind blew strongly from the west.
3. The change from warm to cold weather came without warning.
4. William's record in the Second World War was remarkable.
5. I love to walk through the woods in the winter.
6. We want to write the new words in our notebooks.
7. In some places the wall was wider than it was high.
8. We always visit William once a week.

IV. Phrasing and Intonation

a. *Phrases:* Blend together the words in each of these phrases to form a single unit—that is, pronounce each phrase as though it were a single word. Also stress the accented syllable rather strongly, obscuring the vowels in the remaining syllables accordingly.

a váluable watch	véry wet weather	an ópen window
a wíde valley	a wárm vest	to líe awake
véry hard work	a cóld wind	báckward and forward

b. *Sentences:* The teacher reads each of the following sentences in a normal manner, giving some slight emphasis to phrasing and intonation. Students repeat after teacher. Teacher repeats after students.

1. (Teacher)   Isn't this weather rather⌐warm for winter ?

   (Students) Isn't this weather rather warm for winter ?

   (Teacher)   Isn't this weather rather warm for winter ?

2. (Teacher)   We had to wait⌐three weeks for his answer.

   (Students) We had to wait three weeks for his answer.

   (Teacher)   We had to wait three weeks for his answer.

3. (Teacher)   How long did they⌐stay there ?

   (Students) How long did they stay there ?

   (Teacher)   How long did they stay there ?

Teacher and students continue in exactly the same manner with these sentences: Teacher reads, students repeat, teacher repeats.

4. The weather is warm but the wind is cold.

5. Do you like to walk in the woods alone ?
6. I waited a week for them to fix my watch.
7. William has a new wrist watch which he bought in Woolworth's.
8. What are you watching through that window ?
9. I'm watching those workmen argue with one another.
10. Although Wednesday was a cold, windy day we all went to the wedding.

V. Review Paragraph

One of Rudyard Kipling's most interesting short stories is the story of Wee Willie Winkle. Wee Willie Winkle was a small boy whose real name was Percival William Williams. The word *wee*, of course, is an old Scottish word meaning very small. Wee Willie Winkle was given this name by the soldiers not only because he was small but because he was a great favorite of all the men in the regiment. Wee Willie Winkle wished greatly to become a soldier and he tried to imitate the soldiers in every way possible. But one day Wee Willie Winkle performed a wonderful deed. He saved a woman from capture by war-like natives, watched over her until relief came, and in this way won the well-deserved approval of everyone in the regiment.

f | as in **office, laugh, photo**

I. Production:

Bite the inside of the lower lip with the upper front teeth and blow out, with a voiceless sound.

for	offer	enough
flag	affect	leaf
flat	fifty	loaf
favor	often	roof
photograph	defend	tough
phrase	nephew	wolf

II. Comparison

Practice these contrasting sounds, which are sometimes confused. Repeat several times.

have—half	free—three
save—safe	fought—thought
prove—proof	fan—than
leave—leaf	fat—that

III. Sentences

1. He followed his father's teaching faithfully.
2. You need have no fear of his failing to fulfill his promise.
3. A fire broke out on the fifth floor.
4. A heavy February frost followed the unusually fair weather.
5. Please feel free to correct my pronunciation faults.
6. We all laughed when Fred, who was so fat, fell off the fence.
7. Philip refused to accept his defeat as final.
8. I'll be free between four and five o'clock.

IV. Phrasing and Intonation

a. *Phrases:* Blend together the words in each of these phrases to form a single unit—that is, pronounce each phrase as though it were a single word. Also stress the accented syllable rather strongly, obscuring the vowels in the remaining syllables accordingly.

a góod friend	for a vacátion	hálf and half
between fóur and five	to féel fine	a fréquent visitor
to sáve time	to be góod friends	he's afráid of fire

b. *Sentences:* The teacher reads each of the following sentences in a normal manner, giving some slight emphasis to phrasing and intonation. Students repeat after teacher. Teacher repeats after students.

1. (Teacher)   How has Fred been feeling lately ?

   (Students)   How has Fred been feeling lately ?

   (Teacher)   How has Fred been feeling lately ?

2. (Teacher)   Does the weather affect the health?

   (Students)   Does the weather affect the health?

   (Teacher)   Does the weather affect the health?

3. (Teacher)   Florence and I have been friends for years.

   (Students)   Florence and I have been friends for years.

   (Teacher)   Florence and I have been friends for years.

Teacher and students continue in exactly the same manner with these sentences: Teacher reads, students repeat, teacher repeats.

4. They have both been feeling well recently.

5. The climate of Florida is warmer than that of California.
6. Why is Frances so afraid of fire ?
7. She was burned badly in a fire when she was five years old.
8. We found the future tense far easier to learn than the past tense.
9. The first game finished at four o'clock.
10. Fred will be free after five o'clock.

V. Review Paragraph

Philip Fox was writing a letter to his girl friend Frances Fisher, who lived in Freemont, a nearby town. Philip wrote, telling Frances of his great affection for her. He said that he would follow her everywhere. To be with her for only a few minutes he would suffer the greatest hardships and face the greatest dangers that anyone could imagine. Finally, Philip signed his name, then remembered that he had failed to mention something fairly important. So, in a postscript below his name he added: "By the way, I'll be over to see you on Friday afternoon at about five o'clock—if it doesn't rain."

V as in **vest, of, Stephen**

I. Production:

Bite the inside of the lower lip with the upper front teeth, and make a voiced sound.

vine	clever	love
very	river	leave
vote	cover	give
visit	favor	live
value	flavor	above
vest	never	remove

II. Comparison

Practice these contrasting sounds, which are sometimes confused. Repeat several times.

believe—belief	vests—west
have—half	vine—wine
save—safe	verse—worse
prove—proof	veal—we'll

III. Sentences

1. We all voted in favor of the longer vacation.
2. The governor will veto the bill within five days.
3. We have a fine view of the valley from our front window.
4. We will leave for Virginia at five o'clock.
5. The heavy waves overturned the small vessel.
6. What places will you visit during your vacation?
7. The singer's voice proved to be well above average.
8. Vera wore a long veil which covered her whole face.

IV. Phrasing and Intonation

a. *Phrases:* Blend together the words in each of these phrases to form a single unit—that is, pronounce each phrase as though it were a single word. Also stress the accented syllable rather strongly, obscuring the vowels in the remaining syllables accordingly.

a pléasant voice	the Vólga River	to fáll in love
to líve well	a lóng vacation	a véry sweet wine
néver again	to sáve time	we'll léave soon

b. *Sentences:* The teacher reads each of the following sentences in a normal manner, giving some slight emphasis to phrasing and intonation. Students repeat after teacher. Teacher repeats after students.

1. (Teacher) Why do you never go to the movies ?

   (Students) Why do you never go to the movies ?

   (Teacher) Why do you never go to the movies ?

2. (Teacher) We don't like the movies.

   (Students) We don't like the movies.

   (Teacher) We don't like the movies.

3. (Teacher) Will the President veto the bill ?

   (Students) Will the President veto the bill ?

   (Teacher) Will the President veto the bill ?

Teacher and students continue in exactly the same manner with these sentences: Teacher reads, students repeat, teacher repeats.

4. Have you ever written any verse ?

5. Why did Vera leave school early ?
6. Some friends are visiting them over the week-end.
7. They live in a small village in Virginia.
8. To whom should we give the money ?
9. Give it either to Victor or to Vera.
10. They plan to spend their vacation in Vermont.

V. Review Paragraph

Advertising, as a career, offers variety and a means, very often, of rapid advancement. The advertising writer who can write clever copy and catch the attention of the average reader is highly valued. Very often he deserves the high salary which he receives. Yet this same clever writer must give all of his time and energy to serving a purpose in which he generally has very little interest. He must write with the same interest of such things as victrolas, vinegar, overcoats, ovens, or shaving soap as he would write of more important or vital things. In both cases, he must show exactly the same creative feeling; he must write with the very same enthusiasm. Very often, this proves difficult to achieve. Yet this is the way he earns his living; this is a basic part of the advertising business which he can never, never change.

| θ | as in **thin, author, health** |

I. Production:

Place the tip of the tongue against the cutting edge of the upper front teeth; the breath is then blown out without voice.

thin	method	both
thick	author	birth
thing	wealthy	earth
Thursday	nothing	growth
thank	something	health
theatre	birthday	breath

II. Comparison

Practice these contrasting sounds, which are sometimes confused. Repeat several times.

thank—tank	thank—sank
thin—tin	thin—sin
through—true	thing—sing
thought—taught	thumb—some

III. Sentences

1. Ethel's birthday comes this month.
2. How much is three times three? Three times thirteen ?
3. Thursday is the fifteenth of the month.
4. Thirty thousand soldiers marched through the city streets.
5. Thelma was naturally thankful for the gift of three thousand dollars.
6. She thinks and talks of nothing but the theater.
7. I am through with the thread and thimble now.
8. Our theater tickets were for Thursday, the thirteenth.

IV. Phrasing and Intonation

a. *Phrases:* Blend together the words in each of these phrases to form a single unit—that is, pronounce each phrase as though it were a single word. Also stress the accented syllable rather strongly, obscuring the vowels in the remaining syllables accordingly.

thrée times three	the sáme path	through thíck and thin
on my bírthday	a wéalthy author	to have góod health
héalth is wealth	to thínk of something	nórth and south

b. *Sentences:* The teacher reads each of the following sentences in a normal manner, giving some slight emphasis to phrasing and intonation. Students repeat after teacher. Teacher repeats after students.

1. (Teacher)   The author of that story is Rudyard Kipling.

   (Students) The author of that story is Rudyard Kipling.

   (Teacher)   The author of that story is Rudyard Kipling.

2. (Teacher)   Did Ethel find her thimble ?

   (Students) Did Ethel find her thimble ?

   (Teacher)   Did Ethel find her thimble ?

3. (Teacher)   Where did Thelma put the thermos bottle ?

   (Students) Where did Thelma put the thermos bottle ?

   (Teacher)   Where did Thelma put the thermos bottle ?

Teacher and students continue in exactly the same manner with these sentences: Teacher reads, students repeat, teacher repeats.

4. Is that thunder I hear ?

5. Is Arthur in better health now ?
6. Yes, but three days ago, on Thursday, I thought he was getting sick again.
7. Who is the author of the novel, "The Good Earth"?
8. Don't you think you should thank Arthur for the present he gave you ?
9. We think we will travel through Europe this summer.
10. Anything worth doing at all is worth doing thoroughly.

V. Review Paragraph

The box of thimbles from the Thrifty Thimble Company arrived, as ordered. However, instead of thirty-six thimbles, the box contained only thirty-three thimbles, three thimbles fewer than the thirty-six we had ordered. We wrote to the company, explaining that we had ordered thirty-six, not thirty-three, thimbles, and asked them to send us the extra three thimbles at once. They replied that they were in error in sending only thirty-three thimbles rather than thirty-six and that they would ship us three additional thimbles immediately.

ð as in **the, father, smooth**

I. Production:

Place the tip of the tongue against the cutting edge of the upper front teeth; the breath is then blown out with voice.

the	mother	leather
there	brother	bother
this	neither	with
that	further	bathe
these	whether	smooth
those	father	breathe

II. Comparison

Practice these contrasting sounds, which are sometimes confused. Repeat several times.

they—day	that—sat
their—dare	these—seize
though—dough	those—sews
than—Dan	they've—save

III. Sentences

1. I didn't know whether he was your father or your brother.
2. It was difficult for them to breathe in such cold weather.
3. There is little good leather on the market now.
4. There is another path farther ahead.
5. Although they were lost, neither one was frightened.
6. My brother would rather sleep than eat.
7. You can choose either one or the other.
8. Neither of them noticed that the other was getting tired.

IV. Phrasing and Intonation

a. *Phrases:* Blend together the words in each of these phrases to form a single unit—that is, pronounce each phrase as though it were a single word. Also stress the accented syllable rather strongly, obscuring the vowels in the remaining syllables accordingly.

to báthe the baby	at thát time	my óther brother
with their fríends	shút the door	Is this yóurs ?
dón't bother them	either óne or the other	Thére they go.

b. *Sentences:* The teacher reads each of the following sentences in a normal manner, giving some slight emphasis to phrasing and intonation. Students repeat after teacher. Teacher repeats after students.

1. (Teacher)   Which tie shall I wear, this one or that one ?

   (Students)   Which tie shall I wear, this one or that one ?

   (Teacher)   Which tie shall I wear, this one or that one ?

2. (Teacher)   I don't like either one of them.

   (Students)   I don't like either one of them.

   (Teacher)   I don't like either one of them.

3. (Teacher)   Have you seen my brother anywhere ?

   (Students)   Have you seen my brother anywhere ?

   (Teacher)   Have you seen my brother anywhere ?

Teacher and students continue in exactly the same manner with these sentences: Teacher reads, students repeat, teacher repeats.

4. To whom does that leather bag belong ?

5. Would you rather have this one or that ?
6. Is that Frank's brother with his father ?
7. Where are your mother and father now ?
8. This is the night they always go to the theater.
9. I'd rather discuss this matter at another time.
10. They knew that there was no other path out of the woods.

V. Review Paragraph

Neither of them was there when their brother arrived. He had not bothered to get in touch with them, and therefore neither one of them expected him. When they came home, their surprise at this sudden visit can thus be imagined. Their brother was rather at a loss for words, and they themselves were almost speechless. They then estimated that it had been more than ten years since they had seen each other. It was, indeed, a happy gathering for all of them—and, although much had happened in the meantime, they were together again at last.

d as in **dog, window, could**

I. Production:

Place the tip of the tongue on the gum ridge behind the upper front teeth, then blow the tongue sharply away, making a voiced sound.

day	candy	bed
dog	children	could
die	today	find
door	ready	good
dress	under	had
down	window	hand
dad	garden	heard

II. Comparison

Practice these contrasting sounds, which are sometimes confused. Repeat several times.

dime—time	medal—metal
die—tie	riding—writing
do—to	wading—waiting
down—town	bed—bet

III. Sentences

1. A friend in need is a friend indeed.
2. The name of the druggist is Dudley Davis.
3. I doubt whether he would dare to do such a thing.
4. The child hid under the bed.
5. We made good time on our drive to Detroit.
6. David finally paid the ten dollars he owed me.
7. The Dean talked with Doris about her low grades.
8. That child seldom does what he is told.

IV. Phrasing and Intonation

a. *Phrases:* Blend together the words in each of these phrases to form a single unit—that is, pronounce each phrase as though it were a single word. Also stress the accented syllable rather strongly, obscuring the vowels in the remaining syllables accordingly.

a góod time	dáy by day	Whát's he doing?
from dóor to door	a bríght red dress	the frónt door
móther and dad	they had léft	a cóld drink

b. *Sentences:* The teacher reads each of the following sentences in a normal manner, giving some slight emphasis to phrasing and intonation. Students repeat after teacher. Teacher repeats after students.

1. (Teacher)   Did you hear that loud sound?

    (Students)   Did you hear that loud sound?

    (Teacher)   Did you hear that loud sound?

2. (Teacher)   Yes, it came from the garden.

    (Students)   Yes, it came from the garden.

    (Teacher)   Yes, it came from the garden.

3. (Teacher)   What did you do all day yesterday?

    (Students)   What did you do all day yesterday?

    (Teacher)   What did you do all day yesterday?

Teacher and students continue in exactly the same manner with these sentences: Teacher reads, students repeat, teacher repeats.

4. Do both children always drink their milk?

5. Sometimes they do and sometimes they don't.
6. What did Donald say about his trip?
7. He didn't mention a word about it.
8. Did you read Dora's letter?
9. You went for a long drive today, didn't you?
10. Yes, we got up at dawn to do it.

V. Pronunciation of Terminal Ending ED:

The ending *ed*, when added to any regular verb to form the simple past tense, is pronounced as follows:

1. It is pronounced as a separate syllable [ɪd] if the verb ends in *t* or *d*.

   wait   waited (pronounced *wait ed* [wétɪd])
   want   wanted (pronounced *want ed* [wántɪd])

2. It is pronounced [t] if the verb ends in any voiceless sound (except *t*).

   ask   asked (pronounced *asked* [æskt])
   wash   washed (pronounced *washed* [waʃt])

3. It is pronounced [d] if the verb ends in any voiced sound (except *d*).

   play   played (pronounced *played* [pled])
   turn   turned (pronounced *turned* [tɚnd])

t as in **ten, might, receipt**

I. Production:

Place the tip of the tongue on the gum ridge behind the upper front teeth, then blow the tongue sharply away, without voice.

tea	butter	shirt
ten	potato	but
to	letter	eat
teach	sister	get
table	little	foot
tell	water	fast

II. Comparison

Practice these contrasting sounds, which are sometimes confused. Repeat several times.

to—do	feet—feed
tore—door	bet—bed
toe—dough	latter—ladder
tip—dip	writing—riding

III. Sentences

1. The attack began at ten o'clock and continued all night until dawn.
2. We had great difficulty in locating the origin of the trouble.
3. Tom wrote the letter immediately.
4. The heat within the tent was so great that no one could sleep.
5. The child is too young to tell time.
6. We tried several times to reach him by telephone.
7. The tire had been punctured by a small tack.
8. The cat sat calmly on the top step.

IV. Phrasing and Intonation

a. *Phrases:* Blend together the words in each of these phrases to form a single unit—that is, pronounce each phrase as though it were a single word. Also stress the accented syllable rather strongly, obscuring the vowels in the remaining syllables accordingly.

to gó downtown	bréad and butter	Pút it away.
to féel tired	to téll the truth	téa and toast
líttle by little	a gláss of water	to wríte a letter

b. *Sentences:* The teacher reads each of the following sentences in a normal manner, giving some slight emphasis to phrasing and intonation. Students repeat after teacher. Teacher repeats after students.

1. (Teacher)   What's the matter with Tom today?
   (Students) What's the matter with Tom today?
   (Teacher)   What's the matter with Tom today?

2. (Teacher)   I haven't the faintest idea.
   (Students) I haven't the faintest idea.
   (Teacher)   I haven't the faintest idea.

3. (Teacher)   Haven't you written to your aunt yet?
   (Students) Haven't you written to your aunt yet?
   (Teacher)   Haven't you written to your aunt yet?

Teacher and students continue in exactly the same manner with these sentences: Teacher reads, students repeat, teacher repeats.

4. I really hate to write letters.

5. How much is two times two? Ten times ten?
6. Where is your little sister?
7. She's outside playing with the kitten.
8. Night after night they played their radio until almost midnight.

V. Pronunciation of Terminal Ending ED:

In the previous exercise (page 51), we learned that the ending *ed*, when added to any regular verb to form the simple past tense, is pronounced in one of the following three ways: 1. It is pronounced as a separate syllable [ɪd] if the verb ends in *t* or *d*. Example: *waited* (pronounced *wait ed* [wétɪd]). 2. It is pronounced [t] if the verb ends in any voiceless sound—except *t*. Example: *asked* (pronounced *asked* [æskt]). 3. It is pronounced [d] if the verb ends in any voiced sound—except *d*. Example: *played* (pronounced *played* [pled]).

Now, in accordance with these instructions, pronounce the past tense form of these regular verbs carefully after your teacher. Repeat several times.

ed pronounced as separate syllable [ɪd]	*ed* pronounced [t]	*ed* pronounced [d]
wanted	dressed	lived
handed	liked	mailed
attended	thanked	believed
affected	decreased	contained
added	jumped	cleaned
accepted	noticed	learned
ended	walked	dialed
needed	stopped	explained
decided	worked	followed
excited	picked	imagined
interested	placed	loved

n as in no, window, down

I. Production:

Open your mouth; raise the tip of the tongue to the upper gum ridge, keeping the sides of the tongue touching the inside of the upper teeth. Send the voiced sound through the nose.

no	any	green
name	only	been
new	morning	ran
never	raining	than
noon	window	train
not	into	down

II. Comparison

Practice these contrasting sounds, which are sometimes confused. Repeat several times.

neck—deck	dine—died
nor—door	pan—pad
near—dear	pain—paid
net—debt	train—trade

III. Sentences

1. They need have no fear of our refusing to help them.
2. A number of new applications has been received.
3. I had telephoned him at least nine or ten times.
4. The news that the governor had spent the night in New York was not reported in the newspapers.
5. Though opportunity may knock only once for some people, it seems to knock quite often for others.
6. We received no news from them for nearly a month.
7. The work will be finished by next November.
8. We never know when to expect him.

IV. Phrasing and Intonation

a. *Phrases:* Blend together the words in each of these phrases to form a single unit—that is, pronounce each phrase as though it were a single word. Also stress the accented syllable rather strongly, obscuring the vowels in the remaining syllables accordingly.

a ráiny day	véry noisy neighbors	níght after night
néver again	nóthing at all	an ópen window
láte at night	there's nóne left	níne will be enóugh

b. *Sentences:* The teacher reads each of the following sentences in a normal manner, giving some slight emphasis to phrasing and intonation. Students repeat after teacher. Teacher repeats after students.

1. (Teacher)   Have you ever known such a noisy person?

   (Students)   Have you ever known such a noisy person?

   (Teacher)   Have you ever known such a noisy person?

2. (Teacher)   What color is your new dress—green?

   (Students)   What color is your new dress—green?

   (Teacher)   What color is your new dress—green?

3. (Teacher)   It's raining too hard to go out.

   (Students)   It's raining too hard to go out.

   (Teacher)   It's raining too hard to go out.

Teacher and students continue in exactly the same manner with these sentences: Teacher reads, students repeat, teacher repeats.

4. Ned was nineteen on his last birthday.

5. When did Nathan join the navy?
6. The Nelsons are leaving for Nevada tomorrow.
7. Nora never gets up before noon.
8. Ned takes a nap nearly every afternoon.
9. Did Dan earn any money during the summer?
10. We knocked and knocked but no one answered.

V. Special Intonation Patterns:

Although, as we have learned (page 15-16), the high note in any normally spoken sentence falls on the final stressed syllable, sometimes it is necessary to raise the pitch on some other syllable in order to give emphasis to a particular idea. For example, let us consider the sentence: *When are they leaving for Chicago?* Without any particular intonation stress, the sentence might well appear rather indefinite as to meaning. However, we can convey whatever idea the speaker has in mind simply by raising the pitch on the indicated syllable. Thus—

When are they leaving for Chicago? Accent on time—*when.*

When are they leaving for Chicago? Accent on *are*—perhaps conveying some impatience as to a possible delay.

When are they leaving for Chicago? Accent on *they*—rather than on someone else.

When are they leaving for Chicago? Normal accent on *leaving.*

When are they leaving for Chicago? Accent on *Chicago*—rather than on some place else.

l as in **lady, follow, well**

I. Production:

Place the tip of the tongue on the upper gum ridge, and let the voiced breath come over the relaxed sides of the tongue.

left	believe	all
leave	hello	call
little	only	girl
life	belong	shall
long	follow	will
like	silent	tell
lip	careless	well

II. Comparison

Practice these contrasting sounds, which are sometimes confused. Repeat several times.

lies—wise	long—wrong
let—wet	light—right
life—wife	list—wrist
leak—weak	late—rate

III. Sentences

1. His illness delayed him from completing the work.
2. The law was repealed by the legislature.
3. Her life seemed to be a series of long illnesses.
4. He who laughs last laughs best.
5. Della's umbrella lay floating in the lake.
6. The last line of the poem caused a good deal of laughter.
7. The leaves turn yellow in early autumn.
8. Lake Superior is the largest of the Great Lakes.

IV. Phrasing and Intonation

a. *Phrases:* Blend together the words in each of these phrases to form a single unit—that is, pronounce each phrase as though it were a single word. Also stress the accented syllable rather strongly, obscuring the vowels in the remaining syllables accordingly.

a lóvely girl	Let her alóne.	líttle by little
áll is well	to téll a lie	to líve well
will you wáit?	láte at night	Did he léave?

b. *Sentences:* The teacher reads each of the following sentences in a normal manner, giving some slight emphasis to phrasing and intonation. Students repeat after teacher. Teacher repeats after students.

1. (Teacher)   Would you like to|look at the lake?

    (Students)   Would you like to look at the lake?

    (Teacher)   Would you like to look at the lake?

2. (Teacher)   I'd like very|much|to see the lake.

    (Students)   I'd like very much to see the lake.

    (Teacher)   I'd like very much to see the lake.

3. (Teacher)   Where shall we|meet|for lunch?

    (Students)   Where shall we meet for lunch?

    (Teacher)   Where shall we meet for lunch?

Teacher and students continue in exactly the same manner with these sentences: Teacher reads, students repeat, teacher repeats.

4. Let's meet in front of Lane's Department Store.

5. A little boy just fell into the lake.
6. Will it take long to deliver this merchandise?
7. Laura left a little after eleven.
8. Is Della telling us the truth or telling a lie?
9. Do those letters belong to you?
10. No, they all belong to Louise.

V. Review Paragraph

Late one evening the telephone rang in the office of Dr. L. L. La Plume.

"This is Mrs. Lawrence Lake," a voice said, "I'm sorry, Dr. La Plume, to disturb you at so late an hour. But my child has taken a chill and is quite ill. Our house is a little out of the way, but can you come over right away?"

"I believe so," said Dr. La Plume sleepily. "I have another call to make in that same general direction, so I can call on you both and thus kill two birds with one stone."

r as in **red, right, write**

I. Production:

Raise the tongue and curl it toward the beginning of the hard palate without letting it touch the palate or move while the breath is being blown out with voice.

room	proud	very
run	try	direction
red	tree	marry
ride	drive	story
Robert	pretty	correct
rat	price	favorite

II. Comparison

Practice these contrasting sounds, which are sometimes confused. Repeat several times.

ride—wide	rate—wait
read—weed	run—won
red—wed	rest—west
rent—went	ring—wing

III. Sentences

1. He needs much practice in reading and writing.
2. The river rose several feet during the storm.
3. We were required to take both an oral and a written examination.
4. It has been over a year since he first began work on the book.
5. Ruth hurt her right wrist when she fell.
6. In some languages one reads from right to left rather than from left to right.
7. The view of the river from here is perfect.
8. Every afternoon Richard and Rose go roller-skating in Central Park.

IV. Phrasing and Intonation

a. *Phrases:* Blend together the words in each of these phrases to form a single unit—that is, pronounce each phrase as though it were a single word. Also stress the accented syllable rather strongly, obscuring the vowels in the remaining syllables accordingly.

réady to land	to néed more practice	He líkes to drive.
to wríte a letter	a wíde river	móre than a year
no tróuble at all	a stráight road	right away

b. *Sentences:* The teacher reads each of the following sentences in a normal manner, giving some slight emphasis to phrasing and intonation. Students repeat after teacher. Teacher repeats after students.

1. (Teacher)   When is Richard's birthday?

   (Students)   When is Richard's birthday?

   (Teacher)   When is Richard's birthday?

2. (Teacher)   His birthday is the twenty-third of April.

   (Students)   His birthday is the twenty-third of April.

   (Teacher)   His birthday is the twenty-third of April.

3. (Teacher)   Do you practice these drills on pronunciation?

   (Students)   Do you practice these drills on pronunciation?

   (Teacher)   Do you practice these drills on pronunciation?

Teacher and students continue in exactly the same manner with these sentences: Teacher reads, students repeat, teacher repeats.

4. I practice them whenever I have time.

5. What would you like for breakfast?
6. I'll have orange juice, cereal, and coffee, please.
7. We drove the entire length of Riverside Drive.
8. That's a very pretty dress Rose is wearing.
9. All his answers to the professor's questions were wrong.
10. It has been raining hard all morning.

V. Review Paragraph

Ray's rise to success was extremely rapid. Starting merely as a runner in a Wall Street brokerage house, he worked very hard and soon won promotion after promotion. Finally, he became president of his firm. Then there followed a series of large and rather daring stock market operations, in which Ray took a principal part. His firm grew larger, and his personal power also increased greatly. One read about him frequently in the newspapers, and it was not surprising, therefore, to hear that he had entered politics and planned to run for senator from the state of New York.

S as in see, city, scene

I. Production:

Raise the tip of the tongue to the upper gum ridge and make a hissing voiceless sound.

seat	listen	pass
seldom	lesson	face
same	office	dress
sell	sister	house
saw	cost	lace
smoke	assist	mass

II. Comparison

Practice these contrasting sounds, which are sometimes confused. Repeat several times.

loose—lose	sing—thing
price—prize	sank—thank
peace—peas	sin—thin
place—plays	sick—thick

III. Sentences

1. His assistant sat close by his side throughout the entire meeting.
2. She seldom considers cost when making a purchase.
3. He saved a considerable sum of money while in office.
4. He was saddened by the sudden and unexpected turn of events.
5. They are having a special sale on men's suits at Smith's Department Store today.
6. Yesterday was my sister's first wedding anniversary.
7. Sam went to the post-office to buy some stamps.
8. Sea water is too salty to drink.

IV. Phrasing and Intonation

a. *Phrases:* Blend together the words in each of these phrases to form a single unit—that is, pronounce each phrase as though it were a single word. Also stress the accented syllable rather strongly, obscuring the vowels in the remaining syllables accordingly.

a frónt seat	She's véry sick.	to ásk questions
Thánks very much.	He pássed the course.	the lást lesson
a níce day	What a surpríse!	Did he stáy long?

b. *Sentences:* The teacher reads each of the following sentences in a normal manner, giving some slight emphasis to phrasing and intonation. Students repeat after teacher. Teacher repeats after students.

1. (Teacher)   How many students are there in your class?

   (Students) How many students are there in your class?

   (Teacher)   How many students are there in your class?

2. (Teacher)   There are ten boys and eight girls in the class.

   (Students) There are ten boys and eight girls in the class.

   (Teacher)   There are ten boys and eight girls in the class.

3. (Teacher)   Have you ever traveled through the South?

   (Students) Have you ever traveled through the South?

   (Teacher)   Have you ever traveled through the South?

Teacher and students continue in exactly the same manner with these sentences: Teacher reads, students repeat, teacher repeats.

4. I once took a short trip to South Carolina.

5. Which is more difficult to learn: roller skating or ice skating?
6. Ice skating is much more difficult to learn.
7. Did you have any trouble getting seats for Saturday night?
8. No, I got two good seats in the sixth row.

V. Pronunciation of Final S:

A final *s* is added to nouns in English to obtain plural form; *s* is also added to verbs to form the third person singular form, present tense. Remember that this final *s* is pronounced [s] when it follows an unvoiced sound. It is pronounced [z] when it follows a voiced sound.

Final S Pronounced [S]   *Final S Pronounced* [Z]

(*Nouns*)

books	doctors	oranges
maps	pencils	pears
clocks	teachers	days
hats	trains	hands
months	dogs	windows

(*Verbs*)

eats	comes
takes	goes
speaks	leaves
thanks	arrives

(*Contractions*)

what's	he's
that's	she's
it's	there's

(*Possessive Form*)

Mr. *Smith's* friend	*Henry's* friend
the *student's* book	the *dog's* tail
the *cat's* tail	the *boy's* room

Z as in **zoo, easy, lose**

I. Production:

Raise the tip of the tongue to the upper gum ridge and make a buzzing voiced sound.

zone	razor	as
zoo	result	buzz
Zeppelin	lazy	learns
zebra	museum	does
zoology	dizzy	nose
zero	breezy	was
zinc	loser	rise

II. Comparison

Practice these contrasting sounds, which are sometimes confused. Repeat several times.

prize—price	rise—rice
eyes—ice	pays—pace
to close—close (adv.)	plays—place
to use—use (n.)	lose—loose

III. Sentences

1. The music caused pleasant memories to arise.
2. The zoology class was required to spend the afternoon watching the animals in the zoo.
3. It is always easy to criticize the work of others.
4. The bees buzzed busily around the flowers.
5. She teased her little cousin unreasonably.
6. The cause of the disaster was not easy to discover.
7. The quiz program was easily the most interesting of all.
8. Mr. Jones gave Susan a dozen roses.

IV. Phrasing and Intonation

a. *Phrases:* Blend together the words in each of these phrases to form a single unit—that is, pronounce each phrase as though it were a single word. Also stress the accented syllable rather strongly, obscuring the vowels in the remaining syllables accordingly.

a dózen eggs	Clóse the doors.	He pláys well.
an éasy task	my líttle cousin	She léarns fast.
Does he stúdy?	What béautiful eyes!	He dóesn't dance.

b. *Sentences:* The teacher reads each of the following sentences in a normal manner, giving some slight emphasis to phrasing and intonation. Students repeat after teacher. Teacher repeats after students.

1. (Teacher) Does Hazel study English in your class?

   (Students) Does Hazel study English in your class?

   (Teacher) Does Hazel study English in your class?

2. (Teacher) No, Hazel studies in Mary's class.

   (Students) No, Hazel studies in Mary's class.

   (Teacher) No, Hazel studies in Mary's class.

3. (Teacher) Why didn't you call a physician?

   (Students) Why didn't you call a physician?

   (Teacher) Why didn't you call a physician?

Teacher and students continue in exactly the same manner with these sentences: Teacher reads, students repeat, teacher repeats.

4. Do you often visit the zoo?

68

5. Which do you prefer: classical music or jazz?
6. Generally, I enjoy classical music more than jazz.
7. What size gloves does Daisy wear?
8. Does Charlie find mathematics easy or difficult?
9. Fortunately, he finds mathematics very easy.
10. Who owns that new car across the street?

V. Pronunciation of Final S (continued):

In English, nouns which end in *s* or in an *s* sound (sh, ch, x, etc.) add *es* to form their plurals. Remember that this *es* is always pronounced as a separate syllable; also note that the final *s* is voiced and pronounced as [z]. Thus the ending in every case is pronounced [ɪz].

class—classes [ɪz]	kiss—kisses [ɪz]
bus—buses	wish—wishes
dish—dishes	beach—beaches
lunch—lunches	dress—dresses

Similarly, if a verb ends in *s* or an *s* sound (sh, ch, x, etc.), *es* rather than *s* is added to form the third person singular, present tense. Again, this *es* is pronounced as a separate syllable; the final *s* is voiced and pronounced as [z]. Thus the ending in every case is pronounced [ɪz].

to dress—dresses [ɪz]	to miss—misses [ɪz]
to pass—passes	to brush—brushes
to watch—watches	to catch—catches
to rush—rushes	to cash—cashes

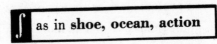

∫ as in **shoe, ocean, action**

I. Production:

Push out the lips; place the front of the tongue on the upper gum ridge and make a voiceless "shh" sound.

shop	fashion	wish
share	ocean	wash
she	election	push
shall	delicious	rush
shoulder	mention	Irish
short	bushel	dish
sheet	depression	cash

II. Comparison

Practice these contrasting sounds, which are sometimes confused. Repeat several times.

short—sort	sheep—cheap
sheet—seat	shin—chin
shock—sock	share—chair
shell—sell	shop—chop

III. Sentences

1. I had no wish to make an issue of the matter.
2. The sheep pushed through the open gate and spread quickly along the shore of the lake.
3. The report clearly showed the position of the ships before the battle.
4. Pushing roughly past us, the man rushed into the shop.
5. She spent her vacation at the seashore.
6. The shelves of the shop were full of old dishes.
7. Mr. Shaw always shines his own shoes.
8. Shirley hurt her shoulder when she fell.

IV. Phrasing and Intonation

a. *Phrases:* Blend together the words in each of these phrases to form a single unit—that is, pronounce each phrase as though it were a single word. Also stress the accented syllable rather strongly, obscuring the vowels in the remaining syllables accordingly.

his lást wish	He shíned his shoes.	to cásh a check
a wásh basin	Did she léave?	púsh and pull
a shórt luncheon	What a sháme!	He rúshed out.

b. *Sentences:* The teacher reads each of the following sentences in a normal manner, giving some slight emphasis to phrasing and intonation. Students repeat after teacher. Teacher repeats after students.

1. (Teacher)   Did you go shopping yesterday?

   (Students)   Did you go shopping yesterday?

   (Teacher)   Did you go shopping yesterday?

2. (Teacher)   Yes, but many of the shops were closed.

   (Students)   Yes, but many of the shops were closed.

   (Teacher)   Yes, but many of the shops were closed.

3. (Teacher)   How often does he shine his shoes?

   (Students)   How often does he shine his shoes?

   (Teacher)   How often does he shine his shoes?

Teacher and students continue in exactly the same manner with these sentences: Teacher reads, students repeat, teacher repeats.

4. I know that he doesn't shine them as often as he should.

5. Why did Sheila wish to leave so early?
6. There was a loud crash as the cook dropped several dishes.
7. Why does Mr. Shaw's hand shake so?
8. We should finish this work by one o'clock.
9. The stock market crash was followed by a national ,depression.
10. The clerk showed Shirley more than ten pairs of shoes.

V. Review Paragraph

The question was whether we should spend our vacation in Chicago or at the seashore. Charlotte wished to go to the seashore where she could fish, watch the ships, and splash around in the water. Shirley was anxious to do some shopping, and so she wished to go to Chicago. Personally, I did not wish to go to the seashore or to do any shopping in Chicago, but I hesitated to mention this fact to either Shirley or Charlotte. After some discussion, we compromised by spending a short time at the shore, a short time in Chicago; then we finished with a week's motor drive through the Shenandoah Valley.

3 as in **usual, pleasure, garage**

I. Production:

Push out the lips, raise the front of the tongue to the upper gum ridge, and make a voiced buzzing sound.

pleasure	treasure	casual
leisure	garage	rouge
decision	usual	confusion
collision	conclusion	persuasion
measure	explosion	provision
invasion	division	excursion

II. Comparison

Note: This particular sound is often a difficult one for the foreign student to produce. The principal fault in making this sound is the substitution of the unvoiced *sh* [ʃ] sound for the vocalized *zh* [ʒ] sound. This results in pronouncing such words as *pleasure, measure,* and *explosion* in a way suggested by the spelling *pleashure, meashure, exploshion.* The student, therefore, must guard against this tendency by producing the *zh* [ʒ] sound with strong voice.

For special practice with this sound, pronounce the following nonsense syllables, laying strong stress on the voiced quality of the first two letters.

zha [ʒa]	zhi [ʒi]	zho [ʒo]	zhu [ʒu]
zha	zhi	zho	zhu
zha	zhi	zho	zhu

III. Sentences

1. The explosion was of unusual force and completely wrecked the garage.
2. He is a casual acquaintance whom I meet occasionally on the street.

73

3. The collision was caused by the poor vision of one of the drivers.
4. We must measure the length and width of the garage.
5. Mr. Mosher suggested a complete revision of our plans.
6. We usually leave our car in a garage on Tenth Street.
7. The collision of the two trains caused great confusion.
8. The decision to begin the invasion at dawn was a wise one.

IV. Phrasing and Intonation

a. *Phrases:* Blend together the words in each of these phrases to form a single unit—that is, pronounce each phrase as though it were a single word. Also stress the accented syllable rather strongly, obscuring the vowels in the remaining syllables accordingly.

too much léisure time	a pléasure trip
during the confúsion	too much roúge
an impórtant decision	to lóok for treasure
an unúsual person	the cáuse of the explosion
a cásual acquaintance	we meet occásionally

b. *Sentences:* The teacher reads each of the following sentences in a normal manner, giving some slight emphasis to phrasing and intonation. Students repeat after teacher. Teacher repeats after students.

1. (Teacher)   Where did the collision take place?

    (Students)   Where did the collision take place?

    (Teacher)   Where did the collision take place?

2. (Teacher)   It took place in front of the Treasury Building.

    (Students)   It took place in front of the Treasury Building.

    (Teacher)   It took place in front of the Treasury Building.

3. (Teacher) <u>Do you enjoy</u>|going on excursions?

   (Students) Do you enjoy going on excursions?

   (Teacher) Do you enjoy going on excursions?

Teacher and students continue in exactly the same manner with these sentences: Teacher reads, students repeat, teacher repeats.

4. Frankly, I have never gone anywhere on an excursion.
5. What does Mr. Mosher do with all his leisure time?
6. He has a workshop in his garage where he usually spends a lot of time.
7. What was the cause of the explosion?
8. The police have not yet reached a decision in the matter.
9. Ask the garage mechanic to measure the oil.
10. I came to the conclusion that I had forgotten to do long division.

V. Homonyms:

Pronounce correctly the following list of paired homonyms. A homonym is a word spelled differently but pronounced in the same way as another word. Also distinguish in meaning between the two words which form each pair of homonyms.

their—there	knight—night	cent—scent
weight—wait	know—no	scene—seen
threw—through	cell—sell	forth—fourth
knew—new	cellar—seller	die—dye
waist—waste	sail—sale	flour—flower
way—weigh	sees—seize	road—rode
weak—week	berth—birth	right—write
wood—would	heal—heel	red—read

t∫ as in **child, cello, adventure**

I: Production:

Raise the front of the tongue to the upper gum ridge and glide the two sounds together in a voiceless sound.

chair	actual	reach
chief	capture	teach
chess	butcher	couch
choice	feature	approach
choose	natural	lunch
cheap	picture	march

II. Comparison

Practice these contrasting sounds, which are sometimes confused. Repeat several times.

chew—shoe	choke—joke
chin—shin	cheap—jeep
cheap—sheep	chin—gin
cheat—sheet	choice—Joyce

III. Sentences

1. Having been permitted to pick out his own present, Chester chose a rich looking gold watch.
2. He also chose a gold chain which matched the watch nicely.
3. The actual capture of the thieves took place only after a long chase.
4. After lunch, we watched a tennis match between Charles and Jim.
5. Mr. Chase is going to teach me how to play chess.
6. The child reached up and touched the chair.
7. We have a cherry tree and a peach tree in our back yard.
8. Don't count your chickens before they are hatched.

IV. Phrasing and Intonation

a. *Phrases:* Blend together the words in each of these phrases to form a single unit—that is, pronounce each phrase as though it were a single word. Also stress the accented syllable rather strongly, obscuring the vowels in the remaining syllables accordingly.

to cátch a fish

ríght after lunch

a chéap pair of shoes

to téach school

a góod teacher

Where's the chéck room?

a prétty handkerchief

Whích is which?

to pláy checkers

to gó to church

b. *Sentences:* The teacher reads each of the following sentences in a normal manner, giving some slight emphasis to phrasing and intonation. Students repeat after teacher. Teacher repeats after students.

1. (Teacher)   How often do they go to church?

   (Students)   How often do they go to church?

   (Teacher)   How often do they go to church?

2. (Teacher)   They go to church each Sunday.

   (Students)   They go to church each Sunday.

   (Teacher)   They go to church each Sunday.

3. (Teacher)   Do you know how to play chess?

   (Students)   Do you know how to play chess?

   (Teacher)   Do you know how to play chess?

Teacher and students continue in exactly the same manner with these sentences: Teacher reads, students repeat, teacher repeats.

4. Yes, but I don't play chess very well.
5. What is the price of these handkerchiefs?
6. These handkerchiefs cost one dollar each.
7. Does your new watch keep good time?
8. No, it's a cheap watch and does not run too well.
9. Who is your favorite teacher?
10. My favorite teacher is Miss Chapman.

V. Review Paragraph

Professor Chase was a good teacher, but a rather strange chap in many ways. Our class met right after lunch, and Professor Chase was habitually late. Each day we would watch the clock carefully, hoping he would not reach the class in time, for we were required to wait only twenty minutes for any teacher, even a full professor like Charlie Chase. One day, although Professor Chase's hat lay on his chair, we waited the required period of time and then all marched out in a bunch at exactly twenty minutes after one.

The next day, Professor Chase was very punctual, reaching class at exactly one o'clock. But he seemed quite disturbed by our actions of the previous day.

"Remember this," he said. "Whenever my hat is on my chair, that is exactly the same as if I were here."

The next day Professor Chase chanced to be late again. As he approached the classroom, however, Professor Chase saw no students present. But each of us had carefully left his hat lying on his chair.

d3 as in joy, magic, cordial

I. Production:

Raise the front of the tongue to the upper gum ridge and glide the two sounds together into a voiced sound.

judge	soldier	wage
jail	subject	damage
joke	enjoy	image
joy	manager	page
jewel	major	edge
jaw	urgent	stage

II. Comparison

Practice these contrasting sounds, which are sometimes confused. Repeat several times.

joke—choke	jet—yet
jeep—cheap	jot—yacht
gin—chin	jail—Yale
jeer—cheer	Jess—yes

III. Sentences

1. The jewelry was found undamaged hidden underneath a bridge.
2. John has been appointed manager of the new travel agency.
3. No one apparently enjoyed the joke as much as Jimmy himself.
4. I read page after page of the manuscript, but with little understanding of the subject matter.
5. General Stonewall Jackson was one of the South's most famous soldiers.

6. Both passengers were injured when the carriage overturned.

7. John enjoyed watching the Japanese jugglers.

8. The village bridge was badly damaged by the heavy rains.

IV. Phrasing and Intonation

a. *Phrases:* Blend together the words in each of these phrases to form a single unit—that is, pronounce each phrase as though it were a single word. Also stress the accented syllable rather strongly, obscuring the vowels in the remaining syllables accordingly.

a májor change	a fámous judge	Who arránged it?
I imágine so	Spéak to the manager.	some rípe oranges
We enjóyed the show.	a trável agency	páge after page

b. *Sentences:* The teacher reads each of the following sentences in a normal manner, giving some slight emphasis to phrasing and intonation. Students repeat after teacher. Teacher repeats after students.

1. (Teacher)   What is that strange noise I hear?

   (Students)   What is that strange noise I hear?

   (Teacher)   What is that strange noise I hear?

2. (Teacher)   The wind in the trees makes many strange noises.

   (Students)   The wind in the trees makes many strange noises.

   (Teacher)   The wind in the trees makes many strange noises.

3. (Teacher)   Did you enjoy the concert last night?

   (Students)   Did you enjoy the concert last night?

   (Teacher)   Did you enjoy the concert last night?

Teacher and students continue in exactly the same manner with these sentences: Teacher reads, students repeat, teacher repeats.

4. Yes, I enjoyed it very much.
5. Do you drink much orange juice?
6. Yes, I drink orange juice every morning for breakfast.
7. Who arranged the flowers in that vase?
8. Julia arranged them. Aren't they lovely?
9. What is your favorite subject at school?
10. Geography has always been my favorite subject.

V. Review Paragraph

There was once a small boy named Jack Jameison, who lived in the village of Jamesville, in the state of Georgia. Young Jameison was judged by some of the villagers to be a little foolish, but he was just as clever as any boy of his age.

One day Jack went to the village store to buy some groceries: some jelly, oranges, jam, and finally, five cents worth of cheese. The storekeeper, Mr. Jenkins, however, objected to selling so small a piece of cheese. Mr. Jenkins said that he just couldn't judge the size of a five-cent piece of cheese.

"Then give me ten cents worth," said Jack Jameison.

Mr. Jenkins then cut a ten-cent wedge of cheese. Jack Jameison laid five cents on the edge of the counter. "Now just cut that piece in half," little Jack said to Mr. Jenkins.

y as in yes, million, amuse*

I. Production:

Raise the middle of the tongue to the "ee" position and force the breath out with voice.

yes	yawn	amuse
year	use	lawyer
you	genius	Italian
yet	onion	Spaniard
young	beyond	Hawaiian
yesterday	opinion	familiar

II. Comparison

Practice these contrasting sounds, which are sometimes confused. Repeat several times.

yet—jet	yes—chess
yellow—jello	you—chew
year—jeer	use—choose
Yale—jail	year—cheer

III. Sentences

1. My traveling companion proved to be a brilliant young man.
2. The goal of a million dollars in contributions has not yet been reached.
3. Daniel is now a junior in high school and next year will be a senior.
4. Year after year she wears the same old yellow hat.
5. It is useless to yearn for things which are beyond our reach.

*See footnote, bottom of page 20.

6. Yesterday Mr. Young finally said "yes" to our request.
7. The population of New York City is about eight million.
8. William's sister is much younger than he.

IV. Phrasing and Intonation

a. *Phrases:* Blend together the words in each of these phrases to form a single unit—that is, pronounce each phrase as though it were a single word. Also stress the accented syllable rather strongly, obscuring the vowels in the remaining syllables accordingly.

a yéllow sweater

yóu and I

a brílliant young man

Yésterday was Tuesday.

You're yáwning.

Do you líke New York?

the yólk of an egg

Yés, I dó.

b. *Sentences:* The teacher reads each of the following sentences in a normal manner, giving some slight emphasis to phrasing and intonation. Students repeat after teacher. Teacher repeats after students.

1. (Teacher)   Who is that child in the yellow dress?

   (Students)   Who is that child in the yellow dress?

   (Teacher)   Who is that child in the yellow dress?

2. (Teacher)   Do they still live in Yonkers?

   (Students)   Do they still live in Yonkers?

   (Teacher)   Do they still live in Yonkers?

3. (Teacher)   No, they moved to New York yesterday.

   (Students)   No, they moved to New York yesterday.

   (Teacher)   No, they moved to New York yesterday.

Teacher and students continue in exactly the same manner with these sentences: Teacher reads, students repeat, teacher repeats.

4. This yellow pencil is yours, not mine.
5. William plans to attend Yale University.
6. To whom does that big yacht belong?
7. It belongs to an official of the Italian government.
9. The yarn which she bought for the sweater was bright yellow.
10. We won't see you again until next year.

V. Review Paragraph

A young boy in a yellow shirt sat in his front yard. He was yawning sleepily. His only companion was an old mule.

A stranger came along. "Is that mule yours?" asked the stranger.

"Yes, Sir," said the young boy, whose name was William, politely.

"He looks a little vicious," said the stranger.

"Yes, Sir," said William. "Sometimes he's a little hard to handle."

"Has he ever kicked you?" asked the stranger.

"Not yet," said William, still yawning. "But he has kicked the place where I just was plenty of times."

k as in **can, keep, character**

I. Production:

Raise the back of the tongue to touch the soft palate. Let it quickly break contact, thus making a voiceless sound.

cat	o'clock	look
can	because	make
call	picture	like
come	American	thank
cool	school	took
cut	escape	walk

II. Comparison

Practice these contrasting sounds, which are sometimes confused. Repeat several times.

coat—goat	rack—rag
cold—gold	back—bag
coast—ghost	duck—dug
come—gum	pick—pig

III. Sentences

1. We walked back to camp a rather sad group.
2. The long climb to the top of the cliff left me weak and breathless.
3. In place of a regular top, we used a piece of canvas as a cover for our car.
4. The king and queen were greeted by crowds of people.
5. The cat plays with her kittens all day long.
6. The cook baked a delicious cake for the party.
7. The ink stained the carpet and we had to send it to be cleaned.
8. We went to Kentucky to visit Cousin Carl.

IV. Phrasing and Intonation

a. *Phrases:* Blend together the words in each of these phrases to form a single unit—that is, pronounce each phrase as though it were a single word. Also stress the accented syllable rather strongly, obscuring the vowels in the remaining syllables accordingly.

to wálk to work	What a cúte kitten!	Thank Káthryn for it.
a cléar day	The dog is bárking.	Cárl can cóme.
to wórk hard	to gó for a walk	Carl cán't come.

b. *Sentences:* The teacher reads each of the following sentences in a normal manner, giving some slight emphasis to phrasing and intonation. Students repeat after teacher. Teacher repeats after students.

1. (Teacher) Can you come at six o'clock?

   (Students) Can you come at six o'clock?

   (Teacher) Can you come at six o'clock?

2. (Teacher) I can but Kathryn can't.

   (Students) I can but Kathryn can't.

   (Teacher) I can but Kathryn can't.

3. (Teacher) What would you like for breakfast?

   (Students) What would you like for breakfast?

   (Teacher) What would you like for breakfast?

Teacher and students continue in exactly the same manner with these sentences: Teacher reads, students repeat, teacher repeats.

4. I'd like bacon and eggs, biscuits, and coffee.

5. Will the cat come if you call her?
6. Sometimes she comes and sometimes she doesn't.
7. How would you like to take a walk?
8. I'm afraid that it looks like rain.

V. Positive and Negative Stress Patterns:

Note carefully that all auxiliary verbs in English are generally lightly stressed. The principal stress in the normal verb phrase falls on the main verb.

In negative sentences, however, the contraction of the auxiliary verb and the word *not* is generally stressed. In fact, this stress pattern helps greatly to signalize negative form. This is an important consideration for the foreign student. In using the wrong stress pattern in such sentences, he will inevitably confuse his listener as to whether he has spoken positively or negatively. As a result, he frequently runs the risk of being completely misunderstood.

Positive Stress Pattern With Auxiliary Verbs

Negative Stress Pattern With Auxiliary Verbs

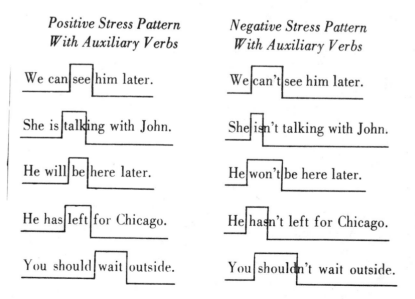

We can see him later.

We can't see him later.

She is talking with John.

She isn't talking with John.

He will be here later.

He won't be here later.

He has left for Chicago.

He hasn't left for Chicago.

You should wait outside.

You shouldn't wait outside.

g as in go, egg, example

I. Production:

Raise the back of the tongue to touch the soft palate. Let it quickly break contact, thus making a voiced sound.

good	forget	big
go	forgotten	dog
get	again	egg
girl	ago	leg
give	together	flag
guess	sugar	dig

II. Comparison

Practice these contrasting sounds, which are sometimes confused. Repeat several times.

good—could	rag—rack
goat—coat	pig—pick
gold—cold	bag—back
game—came	tag—tack

III. Sentences

1. The dog dug eagerly in the ground for the bone.
2. He said he regretted that he could not give her a better recommendation.
3. The game began as soon as the fog lifted.
4. Gertrude cut her finger on a piece of glass.
5. The teacher gave both girls good marks.
6. A dog had dug up all the flowers in our carefully planted garden.
7. Grace is going to the game but Gertrude isn't.
8. They sell good sandwiches in Grey's Drug Store.

IV. Phrasing and Intonation

a. *Phrases:* Blend together the words in each of these phrases to form a single unit—that is, pronounce each phrase as though it were a single word. Also stress the accented syllable rather strongly, obscuring the vowels in the remaining syllables accordingly.

agáin and again	a bíg dog	He cút his finger.
the yóungest son	Trý it again.	bácon and eggs
What a prétty girl!	I cán't go.	a páper bag

b. *Sentences:* The teacher reads each of the following sentences in a normal manner, giving some slight emphasis to phrasing and intonation. Students repeat after teacher. Teacher repeats after students.

1. (Teacher)   Can you go to the game with us?

   (Students)   Can you go to the game with us?

   (Teacher)   Can you go to the game with us?

2. (Teacher)   No, we'll have to get together another time.

   (Students)   No, we'll have to get together another time.

   (Teacher)   No, we'll have to get together another time.

3. (Teacher)   How did you hurt your finger?

   (Students)   How did you hurt your finger?

   (Teacher)   How did you hurt your finger?

Teacher and students continue in exactly the same manner with these sentences: Teacher reads, students repeat, teacher repeats.

4. I caught it in the garden gate.

5. Have you done your English grammar exercises yet?

6. Not yet, but I'm going to do them now.

7. How many girls are there in your group?

8. I don't know exactly. About thirty, I guess.

9. What vegetables grow best in your garden?

10. Asparagus grows well, also green beans.

V. Review Paragraph

A traveler was going through New England, where the natives are sometimes rather unfriendly. For one thing, they seldom talk much with strangers. Meeting a certain villager, whose name was Gabriel Gates, the traveler engaged Mr. Gates in the following conversation:

"Who owns this house?" the traveler asked, pointing to a nearby house.

"Moggs," replied Gates.

"What in the world is it built of?" asked the traveler.

"Logs," answered Gates.

"Any animals hereabouts?"

"Frogs," said Gates.

"What sort of soil have you?"

"Bogs," said Gates.

"How about the climate?"

"Fogs," said Gates.

"What do you live on chiefly?"

"Hogs," said Gates.

"Have you any friends?"

"Dogs," said Gates.

ŋ as in **sing, sank, kingdom**

I. Production:

Raise the back of the tongue toward the soft palate, and make a voiced nasal sound. Do not let the tongue strike the roof of the mouth.

sing	laughing	hungry
bring	coming	English
ring	going	language
long	making	stronger
thing	doing	younger
wing	waiting	angry

II. Comparison

Practice these contrasting sounds, which are sometimes confused. Repeat several times.

tongue—tug	king—kick
rung—rug	sing—sick
wing—wig	lung—luck
hung—hug	bring—brick

III. Sentences

1. We were hoping to get one of the remaining single seats.
2. The men were getting tired of eating such poor food.
3. I had a feeling that we were taking the wrong road.
4. She will try anything to bring attention to herself.
5. A strong breeze was beginning to blow all along the shore.
6. Mr. Kingsley has been hoping to make a living by writing short stories.
7. It had been a long, long time since we had heard such good singing.

8. They have both been studying English since coming to America.

IV. Phrasing and Intonation

a. *Phrases:* Blend together the words in each of these phrases to form a single unit—that is, pronounce each phrase as though it were a single word. Also stress the accented syllable rather strongly, obscuring the vowels in the remaining syllables accordingly.

a lóng time	to gó swimming
He's léaving now.	the Énglish language
I'll be séeing you.	What a thíng to say!
réading and writing	They're bóth hungry.

b. *Sentences:* The teacher reads each of the following sentences in a normal manner, giving some slight emphasis to phrasing and intonation. Students repeat after teacher. Teacher repeats after students.

1. (Teacher)   Are you going to the seashore this spring?

   (Students)   Are you going to the seashore this spring?

   (Teacher)   Are you going to the seashore this spring?

2. (Teacher)   We're planning to go to Europe this summer.

   (Students)   We're planning to go to Europe this summer.

   (Teacher)   We're planning to go to Europe this summer.

3. (Teacher)   Why is the baby crying so?

   (Students)   Why is the baby crying so?

   (Teacher)   Why is the baby crying so?

Teacher and students continue in exactly the same manner with these sentences: Teacher reads, students repeat, teacher repeats.

4. A bee stung her on the finger.
5. Where is everybody going?
6. Everyone's going swimming. Don't you want to come along?
7. No, thanks. I'm not feeling well today.
8. Is the English language difficult to learn?
9. English grammar is easy, but English spelling and pronunciation are rather difficult.
10. I have been trying to reach you all day long.

V. Review Paragraph

One day a young farmer boy by the name of Irving King was riding along through the countryside on his mule. Since the weather was warm and pleasant, young Irving was dozing and dreaming. Then suddenly he noticed overhead a large apple tree, its branches hanging with ripe fruit. He stopped, and, while still sitting on his mule, began picking some of the hanging fruit. As Irving was reaching for a higher branch, however, the mule moved suddenly forward without warning, leaving Irving hanging on to the branch of the tree. The owner of the farm, who happened to come along at this moment, saw Irving hanging there and cried to him:

"What are you doing up there, young man?"

"Nothing, Sir," said Irving a little sadly. "I just fell off my mule."

h | as in **hat, hole, who**

I. Production:

Open your mouth and sigh in a relaxed manner, without voice.

heat	him	behind
have	her	perhaps
hat	hide	anyhow
help	his	behave
hear	who	unhappy
hello	how	ahead

II. Comparison

Practice these contrasting sounds, which are sometimes confused. Repeat several times.

hat—at	hair—air
hear—ear	his—is
hand—and	heat—eat
hit—it	hall—all

III. Sentences

1. The horse had difficulty in hauling the heavy load.
2. The house had not been inhabited for many years.
3. Who told Henry how the accident had happened?
4. Harry had a huge hole in the heel of his stocking.
5. Herbert hurried home because he was so hungry.
6. They built their new home on a high hill above the town.
7. You can hang your hat on that hook in the hall.
8. Mr. Harris had given us no hint of his plan to hire Helen to help him in his office.

IV. Phrasing and Intonation

a. *Phrases:* Blend together the words in each of these phrases to form a single unit—that is, pronounce each phrase as though it were a single word. Also stress the accented syllable rather strongly, obscuring the vowels in the remaining syllables accordingly.

hám and eggs	Have you órdered yet?
It's áll hers	in a húrry
a háppy honeymoon	Whó has it?
What a hígh building!	He's húrrying home.

b. *Sentences:* The teacher reads each of the following sentences in a normal manner, giving some slight emphasis to phrasing and intonation. Students repeat after teacher. Teacher repeats after students.

1. (Teacher)   Why is Helen so happy today?

   (Students)   Why is Helen so happy today?

   (Teacher)   Why is Helen so happy today?

2. (Teacher)   Helen has a new hat and new shoes.

   (Students)   Helen has a new hat and new shoes.

   (Teacher)   Helen has a new hat and new shoes.

3. (Teacher)   Have you ordered your lunch yet?

   (Students)   Have you ordered your lunch yet?

   (Teacher)   Have you ordered your lunch yet?

Teacher and students continue in exactly the same manner with these sentences: Teacher reads, students repeat, teacher repeats.

4. Not yet, but we both want ham and eggs.

5. Why are the children hurrying home?
6. They're hurrying home because it looks like rain.
7. Who is that man in the high hat?
8. That's Professor Harris, the head of the history department.

V. Rules of Accent:

Unfortunately, there are no infallible rules of accent in English. However, there are some general tendencies to be observed. The large majority of two syllable English words—about three out of every four words—are accented on the first syllable. Examples: happy [hǽpɪ], nervous [nɚ́vas], absent [ǽbsənt]. Furthermore, English accent tends to be recessive—that is, it moves toward the first syllable. Take the word *chauffeur*, which was originally a French word and accented on the second syllable— [ʃofɚ́]. Then, as the word became anglicized, the accent shifted, so that today the word is now pronounced *cháuffeur* [ʃófɚ]. Also consider the word *automobile*. Years ago, when the word first began to be used, it was pronounced *automobíle*, with the accent on the last syllable. Later it was pronounced *automóbile*, with the accent on the next to the last syllable. Today it is generally pronounced *áutomobile*, with the accent on the first syllable.

In the following corresponding noun and adjective forms of some common English words, notice how in some cases the accent remains the same in both the adjective and noun forms. In others, it shifts from one syllable in the adjective form to another syllable in the noun form.

Adjective Form	Noun Form	Adjective Form	Noun Form
ínnocent	ínnocence	génerous	generósity
dífferent	dífference	símple	simplícity
póssible	possibílity	régular	regulárity
sympathétic	sýmpathy	suspícious	suspícion
convénient	convénience	mystérious	mýstery
ánxious	anxíety	beáutiful	beáuty

VOWELS AND DIPHTHONGS

i as in **me, beat, people**

I. Production:

Raise the tongue high in the mouth and tense the muscles of the tongue and cheeks. Draw the lips back in a "smile" and make a voiced sound.

eat	these	we
easy	teacher	be
either	meat	she
equal	read	me
evening	deep	three
even	seat	key

II. Comparison

Practice these contrasting sounds, which are sometimes confused. Repeat several times.

eat—it	feel—fill
seat—sit	leak—lick
feet—fit	sleep—slip
he'd—hid	feel—fill

III. Sentences

1. A cool breeze began to blow from the east.
2. Eventually, she will have to economize somehow.
3. After reading for only an hour, I fell into a deep sleep.
4. The sea air seemed to give me new life.
5. She seemed to feel keenly his failure to notice her.
6. Even I had to agree that Stephen was the best choice for committee chairman.
7. A college degree is no guarantee of future success.
8. The priest kneeled and began quietly to speak to the child.

IV. Phrasing and Intonation

a. *Phrases:* Blend together the words in each of these phrases to form a single unit—that is, pronounce each phrase as though it were a single word. Also stress the accented syllable rather strongly, obscuring the vowels in the remaining syllables accordingly.

a bíg field	to féel ill	She'll be láte.
He's stíll sick.	in síx weeks	méat and potatoes
What a déep hole!	an éasy exercise	a góod teacher

b. *Sentences:* The teacher reads each of the following sentences in a normal manner, giving some slight emphasis to phrasing and intonation. Students repeat after teacher. Teacher repeats after students.

1. (Teacher)   Where is Peter working now?

   (Students) Where is Peter working now?

   (Teacher)   Where is Peter working now?

2. (Teacher)   He's working in a steel mill.

   (Students) He's working in a steel mill.

   (Teacher)   He's working in a steel mill.

3. (Teacher)   Do you feel well enough to go out?

   (Students) Do you feel well enough to go out?

   (Teacher)   Do you feel well enough to go out?

Teacher and students continue in exactly the same manner with these sentences: Teacher reads, students repeat, teacher repeats.

4. I feel much better than I did last week.

5. Do you think Edith can fill that position?
6. She seems to feel that she can fill it well.
7. Each day the teacher reads to us some of Keats' poetry.
8. Sheila has been sick for six weeks.

V. Contractions:

Note the following so-called contracted forms. These contractions constitute an important part of English verb structure. They are used continuously in everyday speech. If a person uses the full form rather than the contracted form in speaking, his speech sounds artificial and pedantic. He also destroys the normal rhythm of the sentence, with the result that he may even be misunderstood.

(Positive)	*(Negative)*
I am—I'm	is not—isn't
you are—you're	are not—aren't
he is—he's	
she is—she's	was not—wasn't
it is—it's	were not—weren't
we are—we're	
they are—they're	do not—don't
	does not—doesn't
I will—I'll	
you will—you'll	did not—didn't
she will—she'll	
etc.	will not—won't
I have—I've	have not—haven't
you have—you've	has not—hasn't
we have—we've	
etc.	can not—can't
	could not—couldn't
that is—that's	
there is—there's	should not—shouldn't
what is—what's	must not—mustn't

I as in it, build, been

I. Production:

Raise the tongue high in the mouth. Keep the muscles of the tongue, lips and cheeks relaxed and make a voiced sound.

it	imagine	hill
if	Indian	kill
in	English	bit
ink	his	sit
into	ship	fill
is	rich	fit

II. Comparison

Practice these contrasting sounds, which are sometimes confused. Repeat several times.

still—steel	pill—peal
fill—feel	ship—sheep
hill—heel	bit—beat
lip—leap	sit—seat

III. Sentences

1. His work has improved greatly since last year.
2. It gave him immense satisfaction to be able to compete with the others.
3. He has lived in all of the more interesting cities of the world.
4. The house is situated on the top of a hill.
5. On any clear day, the lake was easily visible in the distance.
6. She seems ignorant of even the simplest facts of English history.

IV. Phrasing and Intonation

a. *Phrases:* Blend together the words in each of these phrases to form a single unit—that is, pronounce each phrase as though it were a single word. Also stress the accented syllable rather strongly, obscuring the vowels in the remaining syllables accordingly.

to spéak English	What a bíg city!	to drínk milk
She's stíll sick.	not quíck enough	to buíld a home
It's dífficult to do.	to fíll a prescription	We've béen there.

b. *Sentences:* The teacher reads each of the following sentences in a normal manner, giving some slight emphasis to phrasing and intonation. Students repeat after teacher. Teacher repeats after students.

1. (Teacher)   Did you have that prescription filled?

   (Students)   Did you have that prescription filled?

   (Teacher)   Did you have that prescription filled?

2. (Teacher)   The doctor said she didn't need it.

   (Students)   The doctor said she didn't need it.

   (Teacher)   The doctor said she didn't need it.

3. (Teacher)   When did Bill leave for Chicago?

   (Students)   When did Bill leave for Chicago?

   (Teacher)   When did Bill leave for Chicago?

Teacher and students continue in exactly the same manner with these sentences: Teacher reads, students repeat, teacher repeats.

4. Is Mildred's sister still ill?

5. Yes, she has been ill for more than six weeks.
6. Where are Bill and Philip going?
7. I imagine that they're going fishing.
8. Is this ring yours?
9. No, that ring belongs to Isabel.
10. Those children drink a lot of milk.

V. Contractions (continued):

In the previous exercise (page 100), we read about the importance of contractions in everyday English speech. The foreign student studying English frequently fails to pronounce these contractions correctly. For one thing, he hesitates to contract sufficiently the two words making up the contraction—with the result that he pronounces many one-syllable contractions as though they were two-syllable words. Study the following and pronounce each contraction carefully after your teacher.

Pronounced as One Syllable		*Pronounced as Two Syllables*
I'm	I've	isn't
you're	you've	
he's	we've	wasn't
she's	etc.	
it's		doesn't
we're	aren't	
they're	weren't	didn't
I'll	don't	haven't
you'll	won't	hasn't
etc.		
	that's	couldn't
can't	what's	shouldn't
	there's	mustn't

ɛ as in **end, any, guess**

I. Production:

Draw back the lips, raise the tongue midway in the mouth and make a short voiced sound.

end	egg	set
any	edge	hen
else	envelope	beg
enter	get	men
excellent	dress	send

II. Comparison

Practice these contrasting sounds, which are sometimes confused. Repeat several times.

pen—pan	set—sit
end—and	well—will
beg—bag	dead—did
guess—gas	ten—tin

III. Sentences

1. He was clever and intelligent but not entirely honest.
2. Helen should make every effort to obtain a college education.
3. A fresh, gentle wind brought us welcome relief from the heat.
4. Many guests had arrived, but there was no one to let them in.
5. The entrance was entirely hidden by a high hedge.
6. He will enter engineering school in February.
7. He was a tall, slender, well-dressed man with rather elegant manners.
8. It was evident that red was Stella's favorite color.

IV. Phrasing and Intonation

a. *Phrases:* Blend together the words in each of these phrases to form a single unit—that is, pronounce each phrase as though it were a single word. Also stress the accented syllable rather strongly, obscuring the vowels in the remaining syllables accordingly.

I guéss so.	a wéll written letter
We mét them later.	a góod friend
an éxcellent idea	Whén will he get back?
You néed a rest.	What térrible weather!

b. *Sentences:* The teacher reads each of the following sentences in a normal manner, giving some slight emphasis to phrasing and intonation. Students repeat after teacher. Teacher repeats after students.

1. (Teacher) What else is there to tell?

   (Students) What else is there to tell?

   (Teacher) What else is there to tell?

2. (Teacher) We've given you every detail.

   (Students) We've given you every detail.

   (Teacher) We've given you every detail.

3. (Teacher) Can you lend Ted a pen?

   (Students) Can you lend Ted a pen?

   (Teacher) Can you lend Ted a pen?

Teacher and students continue in exactly the same manner with these sentences: Teacher reads, students repeat, teacher repeats.

4. There are several extra pens on my desk.

5. The entrance is at the end of the hall.
6. Have you read any good books lately?
7. The child rested his head on Edna's knee.
8. The leaves begin to turn color toward the end of September.

V. Contractions (continued):

We read in the previous exercise (page 103) that the foreign student studying English frequently fails to pronounce many contractions correctly because, for one thing, he hesitates to contract sufficiently the two words making up the contraction. The result is that he pronounces many one-syllable contractions as though they were composed of two syllables rather than one syllable. The principle of rhyme, used in the sentences below, should help to correct this tendency by placing emphasis upon the one-syllable character of the indicated contractions. The student should repeat each sentence several times after the teacher.

1. We pronounce *I'm* to rhyme with *time*.
2. We pronounce *you're* to rhyme with *sure*.
3. We pronounce *he's* to rhyme with *please* or *sneeze*.
4. We pronounce *it's* to rhyme with *sits*.
5. We pronounce *we're* to rhyme with *here*.
6. We pronounce *they're* to rhyme with *care*.
7. We pronounce *I'll* to rhyme with *mile*.
8. We pronounce *he'll* to rhyme with *feel*.
9. We pronounce *they'll* to rhyme with *fail*.
10. We pronounce *I've* to rhyme with *five*.
11. We pronounce *we've* to rhyme with *leave*.
12. We pronounce *they've* to rhyme with *brave*.
13. We pronounce *that's* to rhyme with *hats*.
14. We pronounce *there's* to rhyme with *cares*.

e as in **say, they, mail**

I. Production:

This sound is pronounced just like the pronunciation of the letter "a."

age	baby	day
able	table	may
aim	paper	say
ache	date	stay
ate	same	they
eight	wait	away

II. Comparison

Practice these contrasting sounds, which are sometimes confused. Repeat several times.

lake—lack	late—let
mate—mat	main—men
fate—fat	gate—get
take—tack	date—debt

III. Sentences

1. We'll wait for you in front of the main gate.
2. At this rate, we may complete the work later today.
3. They say that we shall extend aid only to those nations in need of it.
4. The account was paid in full on the stated date.
5. She wore a rather faded, shapeless, gray dress.
6. They may stay here until April or May.
7. The lazy dog lay in the shade of the apple tree all day.
8. They may wait until a later date before making any decision.

IV. Phrasing and Intonation

a. *Phrases:* Blend together the words in each of these phrases to form a single unit—that is, pronounce each phrase as though it were a single word. Also stress the accented syllable rather strongly, obscuring the vowels in the remaining syllables accordingly.

at a láter date	péncil and paper	It's stíll raining.
They've góne away.	What a gáme!	to báke a cake
What tíme is it?	Whát's your name?	a cháin store

b. *Sentences:* The teacher reads each of the following sentences in a normal manner, giving some slight emphasis to phrasing and intonation. Students repeat after teacher. Teacher repeats after students.

1. (Teacher) Can you stay and play another game?

   (Students) Can you stay and play another game?

   (Teacher) Can you stay and play another game?

2. (Teacher) I'm sorry—but it's getting late.

   (Students) I'm sorry—but it's getting late.

   (Teacher) I'm sorry—but it's getting late.

3. (Teacher) How much did they pay for the place?

   (Students) How much did they pay for the place?

   (Teacher) How much did they pay for the place?

Teacher and students continue in exactly the same manner with these sentences: Teacher reads, students repeat, teacher repeats.

4. They paid around eight thousand dollars for it.

5. Have you gained any weight lately?
6. Yes, I've been gaining steadily since my vacation.
7. Do you still go to the same vacation place?
8. Yes, Kate and Mable, in particular, like the place very much.

V. Pronunciation of the Vowel Combination EA:

Unfortunately, English pronunciation often fails to accord with the spelling. Yet certain general tendencies are to be observed. In this book, we are mainly concerned with the pronunciation of individual sounds. Yet, at the same time, we must not overlook the pronunciation of certain vowel combinations such as *ea, ou, ei,* etc. We do not refer here to diphthongs, which are a union or blending of two vowel sounds (See pages 134-142). Instead, we refer to so-called digraphs—that is, combinations of two letters having the pronunciation of a single sound. For example, note below how the digraph *ea* has the pronunciation of three different vowel sounds in the following words:

ea pronounced like the *e* in *see* [si]		*ea* pronounced like the *e* in *bed* [bɛd]		*ea* pronounced like the *a* in *take* [tek]
steal	leave	leather	pleasant	steak
please	meal	ready	instead	break
leaf	dream	bread	weather	great
weak	beach	health	already	
peace	speak	head	thread	
sea	cream	heaven	breakfast	
eagle	clean	red	deaf	

| æ | as in **cat, wagon, laugh** |

I. Production:

Open the mouth, flatten the tongue and make a voiced sound which is not nasal.

aunt	absent	man
apple	ran	example
angry	land	candy
at	laugh	wagon
action	matter	stamp
ask	catch	baggage

II. Comparison

Practice these contrasting sounds, which are sometimes confused. Repeat several times.

bad—bed	hat—hot
sad—said	cat—cot
lad—led	map—mop
land—lend	cap—cop

III. Sentences

1. The avenue was lighted by a series of old-fashioned lamps.
2. He cannot afford to endanger the reputation of his family.
3. The magician made the cat vanish into the air.
4. The accident happened shortly after her arrival.
5. After the examination, we all compared the answers we had written.
6. They began immediately to speak in another language.
7. Marion wore a black hat and carried a black bag.
8. Andrew is studying addition and subtraction in his mathematics class.

IV. Phrasing and Intonation

a. *Phrases:* Blend together the words in each of these phrases to form a single unit—that is, pronounce each phrase as though it were a single word. Also stress the accented syllable rather strongly, obscuring the vowels in the remaining syllables accordingly.

hánd in hand	a dífficult examination
báck and forth	We rán after him.
Have you a mátch?	Have you any bággage?
What a hándsome man!	my lást class

b. *Sentences:* The teacher reads each of the following sentences in a normal manner, giving some slight emphasis to phrasing and intonation. Students repeat after teacher. Teacher repeats after students.

1. (Teacher)   Will Harry be back soon?

   (Students)   Will Harry be back soon?

   (Teacher)   Will Harry be back soon?

2. (Teacher)   He plans to be back by Saturday.

   (Students)   He plans to be back by Saturday.

   (Teacher)   He plans to be back by Saturday.

3. (Teacher)   When is your last class?

   (Students)   When is your last class?

   (Teacher)   When is your last class?

Teacher and students continue in exactly the same manner with these sentences: Teacher reads, students repeat, teacher repeats.

4. My last class is at three o'clock in the afternoon.

5. Have you been asked to the dance on Saturday?
6. Yes, I'm going to the dance with Jack Grant.
7. Dan and Harry are having lunch in the cafeteria.
8. Jack failed to pass his mathematics examination.
9. She plans to spend the summer in France.
10. He who laughs last laughs best.

V. Review Paragraph

The attack began at noon and reached a climax at about three o'clock. Shortly after this, our infantry, led by Captain Andrews, advanced slowly. A gas attack was feared, and each man carried a gas mask. Exactly at four o'clock, however, according to plan, the bombardment stopped, and our main troops attacked. The troops fanned out, and in this manner rapidly approached the enemy lines. The enemy, lacking any assistance, attempted to withdraw, but advance units of our troops were already attacking both their flanks. The enemy thus had little chance to retreat and many were captured. The entire action was accomplished exactly according to plan, and Captain Andrews, who had actually planned the attack, was praised by the High Command for his admirable work.

ɝ as in **her, work, bird**

I. Production:

The sound is the same as saying "err" when at a loss for words.

were	service	first
her	heard	bird
person	work	hurt
earn	word	curly
learn	worse	burn
earth	worst	turn

II. Comparison

Practice these contrasting sounds, which are sometimes confused. Repeat several times.

bird—Boyd	her—hair
verse—voice	were—wear
earl—oil	fur—fair
curl—coil	cur—care

III. Sentences

1. We searched a long time for Pearl's purse.
2. The first and third verses were the most difficult to learn.
3. Earl has worked in that firm for many years.
4. It was early morning when we first heard the cries.
5. Though she worked hard, Gertrude earned little during the summer.
6. John's school work seems to grow worse and worse.
7. Although her purse was returned, the contents were missing.
8. We have had no word from Earl since his return.

113

IV. Phrasing and Intonation

a. *Phrases:* Blend together the words in each of these phrases to form a single unit—that is, pronounce each phrase as though it were a single word. Also stress the accented syllable rather strongly, obscuring the vowels in the remaining syllables accordingly.

wórse and worse	the fírst word	He's stúdying German.
He léarns quickly.	to túrn around	to be óut of work
What a prétty bird!	They were búsy.	He has cúrly hair.

b. *Sentences:* The teacher reads each of the following sentences in a normal manner, giving some slight emphasis to phrasing and intonation. Students repeat after teacher. Teacher repeats after students.

1. (Teacher)   How did Gertrude hurt her hand?

   (Students)   How did Gertrude hurt her hand?

   (Teacher)   How did Gertrude hurt her hand?

2. (Teacher)   She hurt it while working in the kitchen.

   (Students)   She hurt it while working in the kitchen.

   (Teacher)   She hurt it while working in the kitchen.

3. (Teacher)   Are both girls learning German?

   (Students)   Are both girls learning German?

   (Teacher)   Are both girls learning German?

Teacher and students continue in exactly the same manner with these sentences: Teacher reads, students repeat, teacher repeats.

4. Yes, both girls are studying German at the university.

5. Why is Earnest leaving home so early?
6. He's working nights trying to earn some extra money.
7. While stepping off the curb, Earl turned his ankle.
8. Bert served three terms in the foreign service.
9. The first and third words were difficult to pronounce.
10. Mr. Burns hopes to return early next week.

V. Review Paragraph

The Importance of Being Earnest, while not the first of Oscar Wilde's plays, was one of his earliest attempts at comedy. The chief character of the play is a person named Earnest Worthing. The play's title, therefore, is derived from the word *earnest,* Earnest being the name of the hero of the play and at the same time an indication of this person's character. In some ways, however, Earnest was far from being earnest in impersonating an entirely fictitious character. Earnest's life, furthermore, was a rather worthless one. But, as the play proceeds, Earnest turns out to be a fairly likeable person, with no worse purpose in life than to win the hand of the woman he loves.

| ə | as in **cup, love, ago***

I. Production:

Partially open the mouth, letting the tongue rest in a relaxed fashion in the bottom of the mouth. Make a short, voiced sound.

us	love	trouble
up	come	enough
under	some	country
much	son	soda
cut	done	mama

II. Comparison

Practice these contrasting sounds, which are sometimes confused. Repeat several times.

fun—fan	cut—caught
run—ran	but—bought
mud—mad	done—dawn
rug—rag	gun—gone

III. Sentences

1. We were unable to catch either the bus or the subway.
2. Mother was upset when she heard of Uncle's accident.
3. Something must be done at once to help them.
4. He suggested that we go to the country and do some hunting.
5. It was extremely funny to see the umpire standing there on the field holding up an umbrella.
6. The judge cut short the trial and hustled from the courtroom.
7. When the rain started, we all rushed to get under cover.
8. My cousin and I often go hunting in the country.

*See footnote, bottom of page 20.

IV. Phrasing and Intonation

a. *Phrases:* Blend together the words in each of these phrases to form a single unit—that is, pronounce each phrase as though it were a single word. Also stress the accented syllable rather strongly, obscuring the vowels in the remaining syllables accordingly.

a cúp of coffee	a múd puddle	Lét's take the subway.
a drúg store	She cút her finger.	Please shút the door.
He stúdies hard.	I'm nót hungry.	a fúnny story

b. *Sentences:* The teacher reads each of the following sentences in a normal manner, giving some slight emphasis to phrasing and intonation. Students repeat after teacher. Teacher repeats after students.

1. (Teacher)   Have you any money with you?

   (Students)   Have you any money with you?

   (Teacher)   Have you any money with you?

2. (Teacher)   I have some but not very much.

   (Students)   I have some but not very much.

   (Teacher)   I have some but not very much.

3. (Teacher)   What different subjects did the discussion cover?

   (Students)   What different subjects did the discussion cover?

   (Teacher)   What different subjects did the discussion cover?

Teacher and students continue in exactly the same manner with these sentences: Teacher reads, students repeat, teacher repeats.

4. It dealt with some suggestions concerning the construction of a new subway.

5. Don't you want to come to the country with us?

6. I'd love to—but I have too many other things to do.

7. Which do you prefer—the summer or the winter months?

8. I always enjoy the summer months very much.

V. Strong and Weak Forms:

We have learned that in English all words of more than one syllable are strongly accented on one syllable. The remaining syllables, in turn, receive very little stress. In most cases, the vowels in these unstressed syllables are reduced from their normal values to the neutral vowel [ə]. Moreover, many one syllable words, if in unstressed position, are reduced to their so-called weak forms: that is, the neutral vowel [ə] takes the place of the normal vowel found in the "strong" or stressed form of the word. The following is a list of some common one syllable words having typical "strong" and "weak" forms:

Word	Strong Form	Weak Form Used in Normal Speech	
a	[e]	[ə]	*a* big boy
an	[æn]	[ən]	eat *an* apple
and	[ænd]	[ənd]	you *and* I
the	[ði]	[ðə]	on *the* way
are	[ɑr]	[ər]	they *are* busy
to	[tu]	[tə]	go *to* school
can	[kæn]	[kən]	she *can* wait
have	[hæv]	[həv]	they *have* left
has	[hæz]	[həz]	he *has* gone
had	[hæd]	[həd]	we *had* seen it
that	[ðæt]	[ðət]	the one *that* came
was	[wɑz]	[wəz]	she *was* busy

118

| **u** | as in **too, shoe, fruit** |

I. Production:

Round the lips, raise the tongue midway in the mouth and make a long, voiced sound.

soon	soup	grew
tooth	group	crew
movie	move	chew
food	room	blew
shoot	true	flew
school	blue	through

II. Comparison

Practice these contrasting sounds, which are sometimes confused. Repeat several times.

soon—sun	shoe—show
shoot—shut	crew—crow
room—rum	soup—soap
school—skull	noon—known

III. Sentences

1. We were in no mood to go swimming in the pool.
2. The crew could do nothing against the strong wind, which blew from the south.
3. The cool weather caused the flowers to droop and to lose their bright colors.
4. The fact that it would soon be June and there would be no more school pleased all of us.
5. We had a choice of soup or fruit juice for the first course.
6. They are moving to New Mexico in June.
7. Ruth is leaving at noon for New York.
8. It was stupid of him to refuse such a good opportunity.

IV. Phrasing and Intonation

a. *Phrases:* Blend together the words in each of these phrases to form a single unit—that is, pronounce each phrase as though it were a single word. Also stress the accented syllable rather strongly, obscuring the vowels in the remaining syllables accordingly.

Use a táblespoon.	during Júne and July
What a béautiful day!	They'll léave at noon.
What a cúte child!	rather cóol weather
véry good food	Dó your best.

b. *Sentences:* The teacher reads each of the following sentences in a normal manner, giving some slight emphasis to phrasing and intonation. Students repeat after teacher. Teacher repeats after students.

1. (Teacher)   What's the matter with Sue?

   (Students)   What's the matter with Sue?

   (Teacher)   What's the matter with Sue?

2. (Teacher)   She has a bad toothache.

   (Students) She has a bad toothache.

   (Teacher)   She has a bad toothache.

3. (Teacher)   Is your group going to the zoo today?

   (Students) Is your group going to the zoo today?

   (Teacher)   Is your group going to the zoo today?

Teacher and students continue in exactly the same manner with these sentences: Teacher reads, students repeat, teacher repeats.

4. Yes, we're planning to leave around noon.

5. We'll probably spend all afternoon there.

6. When are you moving to New York?

7. We hope to move during June or July.

8. What time do you get through work every day?

V. Homonyms (continued):

Here is an additional list of paired homonyms (See also page 75). You will remember that a homonym is a word spelled differently but pronounced the same as another word. Again, pronounce each word correctly; also distinguish in meaning between the two words which make up each pair of homonyms.

hear—here	knot—not
seem—seam	pear—pair
some—sum	plane—plain
hole—whole	piece—peace
higher—hire	buy—by
him—hymn	role—roll
meet—meat	guessed—guest
made—maid	steal—steel
mail—male	so—sew
in—inn	son—sun
berry—bury	principle—principal
our—hour	dear—deer
break—brake	one—won

U as in **book, full, woman**

I. Production:

Push the lips out slightly, raise the tongue midway in the mouth, and make a short, voiced sound.

good	look	butcher
wood	stood	woolen
would	sugar	push
pull	woman	put
took	bullet	cushion
cook	could	bushel

II. Comparison

Practice these contrasting sounds, which are sometimes confused. Repeat several times.

brook—broke	pull—pool
pull—pole	full—fool
bull—bowl	stood—stewed
could—code	look—Luke

III. Sentences

1. I was sure that he would enjoy such a good book.
2. The woman wore a good-looking wool jacket.
3. She put a cushion under her head, relaxed, and prepared to enjoy her book.
4. She took the sweater, shook it well, and then pulled it over her head.
5. No one was sure which woman in the group had fired the bullet.
6. She was a good cook, but she took little pride in her work.
7. That good looking woman is Mrs. Goodman, the wife of our butcher.
8. The cook never puts enough sugar in her puddings.

IV. Phrasing and Intonation

a. *Phrases:* Blend together the words in each of these phrases to form a single unit—that is, pronounce each phrase as though it were a single word. Also stress the accented syllable rather strongly, obscuring the vowels in the remaining syllables accordingly.

a góod book	a fúll moon	I tóok it with me.
to líve in Brooklyn	púsh and pull	She's a góod cook.
I'm nót sure.	a wool sweater	I wóuld if I cóuld.

b. *Sentences:* The teacher reads each of the following sentences in a normal manner, giving some slight emphasis to phrasing and intonation. Students repeat after teacher. Teacher repeats after students.

1. (Teacher)   Is John a good student?

    (Students)   Is John a good student?

    (Teacher)   Is John a good student?

2. (Teacher)   He would be a good student if he studied more.

    (Students)   He would be a good student if he studied more.

    (Teacher)   He would be a good student if he studied more.

3. (Teacher)   In which part of Brooklyn do they live?

    (Students)   In which part of Brooklyn do they live?

    (Teacher)   In which part of Brooklyn do they live?

Teacher and students continue in exactly the same manner with these sentences: Teacher reads, students repeat, teacher repeats.

4. There is nothing I'd rather do than read a good book.

5. "Look before you leap" is a good motto.
6. The woman stood in the rain for nearly an hour.
7. We all felt sure that she would get sick.
8. We pushed and pulled, but we could not open the door.
9. From which cook book did you get this recipe?
10. Mr. Brooks' hand shook as he signed the contract.

V. Review Paragraph

My fondest childhood memories are those associated with our summer place near Brookline, Massachusetts. There we had a small cabin, which was set deep in the woods. A small brook ran nearby, and there were many cozy nooks in the surrounding woods where, as children, we could play and hide among the bushes. Mother, of course, served as housekeeper, cook, and governess. She was always an excellent cook and could cook almost anything without ever looking at a cook book. She read to us in the evening from good books. She took us for walks in the woods, and looked after us as we waded in the brook. In short, she did everything a woman could possibly do to see that we grew strong and healthy and that our days passed by easily and happily as all good childhood days should.

O as in old, coal, sew

I. Production:

Round your lips and make a long "OH" sound.

ocean	don't	go
over	wrote	know
open	those	show
only	cold	so
obey	home	low
omit	both	snow

II. Comparison

Practice these contrasting sounds, which are sometimes confused. Repeat several times.

note—nut	loan—lawn
home—hum	boat—bought
phone—fun	coat—caught
known—none	low—law

III. Sentences

1. The boys rolled over and over on the lawn.
2. He proposed that all those present state their opinions openly.
3. No notice was given of the closing of the show.
4. He wore an old coat that no one but he would have dared to put on.
5. No one knows where or when he obtained the loan.
6. Mr. and Mrs. Joseph are leaving for Rome in November.
7. You should fold your clothes more carefully before packing them.
8. For a moment Joe did not know whether to laugh or cry.

IV. Phrasing and Intonation

a. *Phrases:* Blend together the words in each of these phrases to form a single unit—that is, pronounce each phrase as though it were a single word. Also stress the accented syllable rather strongly, obscuring the vowels in the remaining syllables accordingly.

The wíndow's open.	What an óld building!	Dón't ever say that.
There's ónly one.	Lét's go home.	The phóne's ringing.
The shów's over.	to rów a boat	óver and over

b. *Sentences:* The teacher reads each of the following sentences in a normal manner, giving some slight emphasis to phrasing and intonation. Students repeat after teacher. Teacher repeats after students.

1. (Teacher)   Did you enjoy the show?

   (Students)   Did you enjoy the show?

   (Teacher)   Did you enjoy the show?

2. (Teacher)   Although the author is well known,
   the play was not good.

   (Students)   Although the author is well known,
   the play was not good.

   (Teacher)   Although the author is well known,
   the play was not good.

3. (Teacher)   Who is the author of that poem?

   (Students)   Who is the author of that poem?

   (Teacher)   Who is the author of that poem?

126

Teacher and students continue in exactly the same manner with these sentences: Teacher reads, students repeat, teacher repeats.

4. I believe that Milton wrote it.
5. Do you ever go rowing on the lake?
6. We go once in a while—but not often.
7. Both boys are going into the army soon.
8. She should not go out in such cold weather.

V. Pronunciation of Vowel Combination OU:

In an earlier exercise, we studied the varying pronunciations of certain vowel combinations—particularly the pronunciation of the digraph *ea* (See page 109). In the present exercise, observe how the vowel combination *ou* may also be pronounced in several different ways. Repeat each of the following lists of words carefully after the teacher.

ou pronounced like the *o* in *over* [óvɚ]	*ou* pronounced like the *u* in *but* [bət]	*ou* pronounced like the *ow* in *how* [hɑu]
dough	cousin	loud
shoulder	rough	sound
soul	enough	out
though	couple	cloud
cantaloup	double	proud
boulder	country	south
doughnut	trouble	found
although	serious	amount
	nervous	around
	dangerous	house
	tough	about

ɔ as in **all, long, caught**

I. Production:

A low, mid-back tongue position; the lips are tense and protruded.

almost	author	fought
fall	although	bought
walk	always	draw
small	also	taught
law	salt	saw
autumn	hall	cough

II. Comparison

Practice these contrasting sounds, which are sometimes confused. Repeat several times.

walk—woke	ball—bowl
law—low	called—cold
saw—sew	bought—boat
call—coal	hall—hole

III. Sentences

1. A large audience listened to the auctioneer.
2. We saw a shawl lying in the hallway.
3. Paul has a bad cough which he caught while swimming.
4. We altered our plans and decided to walk rather than to go by automobile.
5. It was obvious to all that the law must be withdrawn.
6. In his audit of the books, the auditor caught many errors.
7. The ball struck Paul on the jaw.
8. We saw a tall man crawling under our automobile.

IV. Phrasing and Intonation

a. *Phrases:* Blend together the words in each of these phrases to form a single unit—that is, pronounce each phrase as though it were a single word. Also stress the accented syllable rather strongly, obscuring the vowels in the remaining syllables accordingly.

I cáught cold.	He has a bád cough.	a páwn shop
to táke a walk	What a táll man!	Did anyone cáll?
to fáll over something	We sáw them leave.	a fámous author

b. *Sentences:* The teacher reads each of the following sentences in a normal manner, giving some slight emphasis to phrasing and intonation. Students repeat after teacher. Teacher repeats after students.

1. (Teacher) Where is Paul's daughter?

   (Students) Where is Paul's daughter?

   (Teacher) Where is Paul's daughter?

2. (Teacher) She's sitting at the end of the hall.

   (Students) She's sitting at the end of the hall.

   (Teacher) She's sitting at the end of the hall.

3. (Teacher) Have you ever been abroad?

   (Students) Have you ever been abroad?

   (Teacher) Have you ever been abroad?

Teacher and students continue in exactly the same manner with these sentences: Teacher reads, students repeat, teacher repeats.

4. I spent a few weeks in Austria just before the war.

5. Who is the author of that story?
6. The story was written by Nathaniel Hawthorne.
7. Who is going to teach that course during August?
8. Miss Ball taught it last August.
9. Paul should not talk that way about Walter.
10. The Music Hall always draws a large audience.

V. Review Paragraph

Yesterday, we all visited an auction on Alder Street, not far from the Music Hall, and were much amused at the awkward gestures and unusual voice of the auctioneer. The auction took place in a pawn shop, where all kinds of objects which had been pawned were being offered at auction. There was a Spanish shawl and several Mexican objects, made of straw, which we liked. The auctioneer himself was a tall, rather foreign looking man with hair which was almost auburn in color. The audience always applauded his remarks although, frankly, we all thought them awfully stupid. In the end, we bought nothing at all, and finally walked out of the store. However, since it was autumn and the leaves were turning color, we decided to walk as far as the park.

a as in **army, father, guard**

I. Production:

The sound is the same as the exclamation "AHH!"

artist	honor	problem
architect	honest	not
arm	chocolate	far
art	garden	hot
are	politics	bomb
army	popular	Tom

II. Comparison

Practice these contrasting sounds, which are sometimes confused. Repeat several times.

not—nut	cot—cat
shot—shut	mop—map
cop—cup	hot—hat
fond—fund	cop—cap

III. Sentences

1. A long line of palms stood as if guarding the entrance to the park.
2. The charges against Arthur were proven to be largely false.
3. The dog gave a sharp bark, and then sprang at Tom.
4. Though a good driver, Father was never able to park the car well.
5. The argument started when the guard refused them entrance.
6. The architect is planning to start work on the garden next week.

7. The yard was so dark that Carl was almost afraid to cross it alone.

8. Don is rather artistic and hopes some day to become an architect.

IV. Phrasing and Intonation

a. *Phrases:* Blend together the words in each of these phrases to form a single unit—that is, pronounce each phrase as though it were a single word. Also stress the accented syllable rather strongly, obscuring the vowels in the remaining syllables accordingly.

an hónest fellow	to párk the car	Dón't tell Tom.
to gó shopping	to árgue about politics	a sérious problem
What a hót day!	a héart attack	Are they at hóme?

b. *Sentences:* The teacher reads each of the following sentences in a normal manner, giving some slight emphasis to phrasing and intonation. Students repeat after teacher. Teacher repeats after students.

1. (Teacher)   Where is your father, Tom?

   (Students)   Where is your father, Tom?

   (Teacher)   Where is your father, Tom?

2. (Teacher)   He's in the barn with Carl.

   (Students)   He's in the barn with Carl.

   (Teacher)   He's in the barn with Carl.

3. (Teacher)   Are you fond of modern art?

   (Students)   Are you fond of modern art?

   (Teacher)   Are you fond of modern art?

Teacher and students continue in exactly the same manner with these sentences: Teacher reads, students repeat, teacher repeats.

4. Not particularly. Are you?
5. What are they arguing about so loudly?
6. They are arguing about politics—as usual.
7. Mr. and Mrs. Armstrong own a farm not far from town.
8. The lock on my car door does not work properly.

V. Silent Letters:

Many words in English contain letters which are silent—that is, not pronounced. Pronounce each of the following words carefully after your teacher. Also indicate which letter (or letters) is silent in each word.

knife	build	answer
knee	scissors	doubt
handsome	calf	guard
honest	wrong	climb
knew	wrist	thumb
neighbor	listen	honor
knock	sword	walk
Wednesday	guilty	talk
kneel	whole	guest
scene	dumb	aisle
know	half	ghost
guarantee	island	czar

aɪ as in **dry, eye, buy**

I. Production:

This is a diphthong, a combination of the sound [a] as in *father* and the sound [ɪ] as in *city*.

I	time	by
eye	night	my
ice	like	sigh
aisle	dime	lie
idea	quite	die
island	quiet	pie

II. Comparison

Practice these contrasting sounds, which are sometimes confused. Repeat several times.

tie—toy	time—team
aisle—oil	mine—mean
buy—boy	by—be
tile—toil	pie—pea

III. Sentences

1. The island is well isolated and difficult to reach—especially at night.
2. His poor eyesight made it useless for him to try for the prize.
3. Each item which you buy is itemized on the monthly bill.
4. Mr. Wright was so frightened that he dropped both knife and rifle and ran away.
5. Ira is a fine fellow with very high ideals.
6. Irene and Ida sat side by side throughout the entire meeting.

IV. Phrasing and Intonation

a. *Phrases:* Blend together the words in each of these phrases to form a single unit—that is, pronounce each phrase as though it were a single word. Also stress the accented syllable rather strongly, obscuring the vowels in the remaining syllables accordingly.

a fíne night	What tíme is it?	a knífe and a fork
a bríght boy	It's álmost five.	níne or ten times
quíte a while	What a quíet spot!	to sít side by side

b. *Sentences:* The teacher reads each of the following sentences in a normal manner, giving some slight emphasis to phrasing and intonation. Students repeat after teacher. Teacher repeats after students.

1. (Teacher)   What kind of ice cream shall I buy?

   (Students)   What kind of ice cream shall I buy?

   (Teacher)   What kind of ice cream shall I buy?

2. (Teacher)   Vanilla goes well with apple pie.

   (Students)   Vanilla goes well with apple pie.

   (Teacher)   Vanilla goes well with apple pie.

3. (Teacher)   Is Irene younger than her sister?

   (Students)   Is Irene younger than her sister?

   (Teacher)   Is Irene younger than her sister?

Teacher and students continue in exactly the same manner with these sentences: Teacher reads, students repeat, teacher repeats.

4. I believe that Irene is older than Ida.

5. What time is it, please?
6. It's exactly five o'clock by my watch.
7. It's a lovely night. Let's go for a ride somewhere.
8. How about driving to Long Island?

V. Pronunciation of Final Voiced Consonants:

In some languages, voiced consonants, when they come at the end of a word, are automatically unvoiced. In English, however, all final voiced consonants are held and voiced (unless assimilated to a previous sound). In many cases the meaning of almost identical words is determined simply by the voicing or unvoicing of the final consonant. Note one further fact of importance: When any vowel in English precedes a final voiced consonant, it is held longer than when it precedes a final unvoiced consonant. The vowel [æ] in the word *bag*, for example, is held slightly longer than the same vowel in *back*. The vowel [ɪ] in *pig* is held longer than the same vowel in *pick*—etc.

Final Consonant Voiced	*Final Consonant Unvoiced*
bag	back
pig	pick
tag	tack
heard	hurt
need	neat
add	at
had	hat
ride	right
rode	wrote
spend	spent
build	built
said	set
lend	lent

aʊ as in cow, our, house

I. Production:

This is a diphthong, a combination of the sound [ɑ] as in *father* and the sound [ʊ] as in *book*.

our	about	how
hour	around	cow
ourselves	down	now
out	house	town
outside	found	allow

II. Comparison

Practice these contrasting sounds, which are sometimes confused. Repeat several times.

town—ton	now—no
found—fun	loud—load
down—done	found—phoned
shout—shut	town—tone

III. Sentences

1. Mr. Brown was not allowed by his doctor to go out of the house.

2. The crowd let out a howl when the referee gave his decision.

3. No one knows how the mouse got into the house.

4. He spent hour after hour in the garden among his flowers.

5. Howard felt very proud when he was pointed out as the founder of the society.

6. The dog ran around and around the house barking wildly.

7. Since cloudy weather with showers was predicted, we decided not to go to town.

8. Those dark clouds are definitely moving toward the south.

IV. Phrasing and Intonation

a. *Phrases:* Blend together the words in each of these phrases to form a single unit—that is, pronounce each phrase as though it were a single word. Also stress the accented syllable rather strongly, obscuring the vowels in the remaining syllables accordingly.

a póund and a half	to pláy outside	There's nó need to shout.
to búy a house	to fínd out	Lét's go downtown.
We cáught a mouse.	nów and then	nórth and south

b. *Sentences:* The teacher reads each of the following sentences in a normal manner, giving some slight emphasis to phrasing and intonation. Students repeat after teacher. Teacher repeats after students.

1. (Teacher)   How much time must I allow to go downtown?

   (Students)   How much time must I allow to go downtown?

   (Teacher)   How much time must I allow to go downtown?

2. (Teacher)   It will take you at least an hour.

   (Students)   It will take you at least an hour.

   (Teacher)   It will take you at least an hour.

3. (Teacher)   Is Mrs. Brown a good housekeeper?

   (Students)   Is Mrs. Brown a good housekeeper?

   (Teacher)   Is Mrs. Brown a good housekeeper?

Teacher and students continue in exactly the same manner with these sentences: Teacher reads, students repeat, teacher repeats.

4. Why is the crowd shouting so wildly?

138

5. They want the author to take another bow.

6. How did Howard get that cut over his eyebrow?

7. He fell just now as he was getting out of his car.

8. How did you find out in which house they lived?

V. Addition of Final E To Certain Words:

Note how the addition of final *e* to the words in the first and third columns below changes completely the pronunciation of the preceding vowel, even though this final *e* is not pronounced in any of the words. The meaning of the word, of course, also changes. Pronounce each pair of words—that is, the word without final *e* and the word containing final *e*—carefully after your teacher.

car—care	rid—ride
far—fare	plan—plane
bar—bare	shin—shine
win—wine	hat—hate
cap—cape	pan—pane
cloth—clothe	can—cane
breath—breathe	pin—pine
dim—dime	at—ate
rat—rate	pal—pale
star—stare	not—note
fat—fate	quit—quite
ton—tone	spin—spine

ɔI | as in **oil, employ, boy**

I. Production:

This is a diphthong, a combination of the sound of [ɔ] as in *automobile* and the sound [ɪ] as it *city*.

boil	broil	voice
soil	poison	choice
coin	voyage	destroy
oyster	appoint	noisy
spoil	noise	boy
royal	point	employ

II. Comparison

Practice these contrasting sounds, which are sometimes confused. Repeat several times.

oil—earl	boil—ball
coil—curl	coil—call
voice—verse	oil—all
oily—early	toil—tall

III. Sentences

1. The strong smell of oil throughout the voyage was most annoying.
2. We could hear the boys' voices but could not locate the boys themselves.
3. During our voyage to England, we hope to see the Royal Family.
4. Those boys seem particularly noisy today.
5. He has a pleasant voice and hopes to get employment as a radio announcer.
6. The ancient city of Troy was destroyed during the Trojan War.

7. We had no other choice but to send them another invoice.
8. Joyce and Floyd have both been employed in that firm for many years.

IV. Phrasing and Intonation

a. *Phrases:* Blend together the words in each of these phrases to form a single unit—that is, pronounce each phrase as though it were a single word. Also stress the accented syllable rather strongly, obscuring the vowels in the remaining syllables accordingly.

a lóng voyage	the sméll of oil
the bóys' voices	Avóid any excitement.
What a nóisy crowd!	the Róyal Family
We had bróiled steak.	to póint out
the effécts of the poison	a pléasant voice

b. *Sentences:* The teacher reads each of the following sentences in a normal manner, giving some slight emphasis to phrasing and intonation. Students repeat after teacher. Teacher repeats after students.

1. (Teacher)   Did you enjoy your voyage to Europe?

   (Students) Did you enjoy your voyage to Europe?

   (Teacher)   Did you enjoy your voyage to Europe?

2. (Teacher)   We enjoyed it very much, thank you.

   (Students) We enjoyed it very much, thank you.

   (Teacher)   We enjoyed it very much, thank you.

3. (Teacher)   When did Floyd join your club?

   (Students) When did Floyd join your club?

   (Teacher)   When did Floyd join your club?

Teacher and students continue in exactly the same manner with these sentences: Teacher reads, students repeat, teacher repeats.

4. He joined shortly after his appointment as treasurer.
5. I see no point in avoiding them any longer.
6. Personally, I don't like oysters in any form: raw, boiled, or broiled.
7. Roy really spoiled the party by being so noisy all afternoon.
8. The boys refused to join the girls in singing hymns.

V. Rules of Accent (continued):

As mentioned earlier, there are no infallible rules of accent in English. (See page 96). Yet some general tendencies may be observed. Note, for example, that the opposites of many words in English are formed by the addition of various Latin prefixes. The accent in the word containing such a prefix generally falls on this prefix. Repeat the words below after your teacher.

attractive—únattractive
advantage—dísadvantage
fortunate—únfortunate
polite—ímpolite
correct—íncorrect
furnished—únfurnished
kind—únkind
satisfied—díssatisfied
pleasant—únpleasant
dependent—índependent
believable—únbelievable
happy—únhappy

fair—únfair
convenient—ínconvenient
agreeable—dísagreeable
to pronounce—míspronounce
to connect—dísconnect
to continue—díscontinue
to understand—mísunderstand
to button—únbutton
to agree—dísagree
to approve—dísapprove
to obey—dísobey
to inherit—dísinherit

142